Dust
Net

The Future of Surveillance, Privacy, and Communication: Why Drones Are Just the Beginning

by

David Dvorkin

Table of Contents

INTRODUCTION 5

1 DIMINISHING DRONES 9
    The Global Spread of Drones 13
    A Drone in Every Corporation and Government Agency 17
    A Drone in Every Garage 19
    Good Drones in the Air, on the Land, and in the Sea 21
    Looking Ahead 24
    Insects at War 34
    Political Consequences 37

A Bad Summer for Insects 41

2 DIMINISHING PRIVACY 47
    A Tsunami of Data 47
    Coming Soon to a Spy Camera Near You 57

3 DIMINISHING COMMUNICATIONS 65
    Throttling the Web 66
    Drones As WiFi Hotspots 71
    The Coming Age of Communication 75
    Everyone an Eavesdropper 81
    Attacking the Public Internet 82

I Didn't See Anything about It Online 85

4 DIMINISHING COMPUTERS 87
    Power Supply 96
    Sound and Video 98

Data Storage 101

The Best Smart Phone Ever **105**

5 DUST NET WORLD **109**
Smart Dust 111
Motive Power 115
Dust and Other Nets 118
Weaponization 124
Countermeasures 126
Rossum's Universal Robots 137
Private Lives 141

John and Mary, Alone at Last **147**

6 AFTERTHOUGHTS **153**
Emergent Behavior 153
Alien Net 154
Other Avenues 158
The Final Destination 161

REFERENCES **163**

ABOUT THE AUTHOR **189**

INTRODUCTION

For thousands of years, we humans have associated walls with privacy. No matter how primitive our hovel, once inside it we are safe from the eyes and — if we keep our voices low enough — the ears of others.

For ages before that, long before our ancestors had evolved to be human beings, an individual could avoid observation by other members of the group by simply distancing himself physically from them.

In both cases, privacy was gained but communication with others was lost.

All of this is ingrained in our natures and in the structure of our societies, but rushing upon us is a future in which privacy will be nonexistent and communication will be ubiquitous.

Privacy and communication are two sides of the same coin. Increase one and you decrease the other. Until now, at any given moment, we have generally been able to choose one over the other, to choose the one that is more important to us. That choice is about to disappear.

It would be more accurate to say that it's already disappearing. Moreover, thanks to advancing technology and deteriorating legal barriers, the change is happening at an increasing rate.

Drones, those small, remotely controlled airplanes that we used to associate with America's ill-advised wars in dry, dusty, distant countries, have come home. In those far-off wars, drones are used both to spy and to assassinate. At home, in the hands of civilian law-enforcement, they are used only to spy — thus far.

The use of drones has already spread beyond law enforcement and into the private sector, and it is about to spread much further. At the same time, drones are steadily becoming smaller, cheaper, and harder to detect. Legal and social barriers to their use are dwindling.

Separately, electronic communication — the Internet, and mobile devices such as cell phones that can connect to the Internet — is becoming more important, more nearly ubiquitous, and increasingly under attack by governments and corporations. People everywhere want to be able to communicate with friends and relatives and to get reliable information about the world. Governments and corporations have a vested interest in controlling what information people get, especially about the world. Whether it's the government of China wanting to suppress discussion of the Tiananmen Square uprising or a giant oil company wanting to suppress news about a pipeline rupture destroying a forest in Alaska, those in power want to be able to halt traffic on the Information Superhighway at will. This attempt at control inevitably produces resistance and a fight to keep communication free and widely available.

Heretofore, governments and corporations had the advantage regarding both control of electronic channels of communication and surveillance of individuals. That's about to change. The pushback against control of the channels of communication, and the growing availability of cheap, tiny surveillance devices, are about to merge.

This will represent a giant step, an immense change, not so much technically as socially. The social and personal implications are enormous. Everything we have known and believed about privacy and communication for thousands upon thousands of years will cease to be true.

All of this will happen very soon with the advent of what I call Dust Net.

1
DIMINISHING DRONES

When I say that drones are diminishing, unfortunately I don't mean that their use is diminishing. Quite the contrary. Their use, their numbers, their types, their capabilities, and the number of countries and companies producing them are all increasing rapidly. Their size, however, is diminishing. In the long run, this decrease in size is the important story.

The word *drone* generally refers to a small, remotely controlled aircraft used for surveillance or assassination. The formal name for these devices is Unmanned Aerial Vehicle, or UAV.

Most of us first became aware of drones a few years ago, when news reports started telling of attacks by US military drones on members of the Taliban and al Qaeda in Afghanistan during the presidency of George W. Bush. However, drones have been in use since long before the dismal Dubya years. In a sense, they even predate aircraft.

In 1849, the Austrian army used unmanned balloons loaded with bombs to attack Venice. The balloons were supposed to float over Venice and then drop down into the city, along with their bombs. Unfortunately, the wind changed, and some of the balloons drifted back and attacked the Austrians. A few years later, during the American Civil War, both sides tried using similar balloons to attack each other, with similarly unpleasant results. Nineteenth–century armies loved the idea of dropping bombs on the enemy remotely, but clearly balloons were not the answer.

With the advent of airplanes, a more effective avenue appeared. Radio–controlled aircraft were developed during World War One, but they weren't ready to use by the time the war ended. Research continued after hostilities concluded.

World War Two meant another big advance in the technology. Germany produced the famous V–1, a flying bomb they aimed at England. In England, they called it the Buzz Bomb, a curiously friendly name for a weapon of terror.

The V–1 flew until it ran out of fuel. Then it fell to ground and exploded. It killed hundreds of civilians and injured tens of thousands, but perhaps its greatest value lay in its psychological effect. Decades later, my mother, who lived through the Blitz, still remembered vividly the instructions over the radio: Listen for the sound of the Buzz Bomb's engine. As long as you can hear the sound, the weapon isn't a threat. When the sound stops, you have till the count of three to find cover.

German engineers moved on to the V–2, a rocket bomb rather than a flying bomb. Not only was it more destructive than the V–1, it was even more terrifying, because it flew at supersonic speeds. That is, it flew ahead of its own sound and thus arrived at its target silently.

But the V–2 was a divergence from the development of drones. It was the precursor of the nuclear–tipped ICBMs whose existence terrified the world during the Cold War. It was also the precursor of the rockets used to put men in space.

Drone technology continued to advance separately, especially on the Allied side. After World War Two, the capabilities and number of American drones increased greatly, but the emphasis was on surveillance, not on the use of drones as a weapon.

The United States began using drones as assassination weapons in 2001 in the Middle East. The use of US drones in the Middle East, Afghanistan, and Pakistan has been increasing rapidly ever since. They are used to kill individuals and also to destroy equipment such as vehicles.

These modern drones are large and powerful weapons. The Reaper drone, the one favored by the US Air Force and the CIA for use in Afghanistan and Pakistan, is 36 feet long with a 65–foot wingspan. When fully fueled and loaded for takeoff, it can weigh over 10,000 pounds, with almost 4,000 lbs. of that being weapons: air–to-ground missiles and laser–guided bombs. Air–to–air missiles will probably be added soon. It cruises at 25,000 feet and can go as high as 50,000 feet, and it can hit a top speed of 300 mph. It can stay in the air for 14 hours.

The appeal of these undetectable, unstoppable weapons that can fly just about anywhere and kill a presumed enemy without exposing US personnel to danger is obvious. The moral dilemmas their use entails, the anger of foreign nations at the disregard for their sovereignty, the danger of killing innocent people by mistake, the probability that drones will be used for assassinations whose motivation is political and not military — these are also obvious.

Almost certainly, our drones have already killed innocent people by mistake. An NBC News review of classified intelligence reports has revealed that the CIA often does not know whom its drones are killing. Nor does it know if the people on the ground targeted for death by drone are really militants or enemies of the United States. Reports by locals indicate that many of the victims of drone attacks are innocent civilians. Some targets are chosen because they have been identified as known enemies. Others are chosen because of patterns of behavior. A group or gathering may trigger an alert because it seems to match the pattern of meetings of militants. We've all read the reports of large numbers of people attending weddings or funerals being killed by American drones. Presumably they gathered in just the wrong way. [1]

Discussions of drones and the dangers inherent in their use tend to emphasize their speed and firepower. That's understandable when the discussion is focused on drones as an advanced type of offensive weapon. Size and power are good attributes for a weapon designed to kill people and destroy vehicles and buildings.

But there's another role for drones, a more important one in the long run, and in that role, size is a disadvantage.

That role is surveillance and information gathering. For drones designed for those purposes, the smaller, the better.

Research and development is progressing rapidly in both directions. Weaponized drones are becoming ever more fearsome weapons of war. At the same time, governments and private entities all over the world are making steady progress in the creation of ever smaller drones with ever greater information-gathering capabilities.

Moreover, the use of drones has already spread beyond law enforcement and into the private sector, and it is about to spread much further.

The Global Spread of Drones

We in the United States may think that we alone possess powerful drones and that we're safe from dangerous drones in the hands of our enemies. Anyone who thinks that is naïve. Recall that drones were not invented in the USA. Continued development of more powerful drones since those early days has not been limited to the United States — or Israel, the next major power in the production of drones after the US.

China, unsurprisingly, is working hard to catch up with the US and Israel. China is still well behind the two leaders, but it's making rapid progress. Despite the intelligence resources that the United States and others no doubt employ in watching China's military progress, the West was surprised at the variety and capabilities of drones unveiled at Air Show 2010 in Zhuhai, southern China in November 2010. The new models of drone included one powered by a jet engine. That drone should be able to fly faster than America's Reaper drones. China has already considered using its drones to eliminate a drug trafficker in a neighboring country. As China achieves superpower status, it will feel no more hesitation to use its drones anywhere in the world than the US does. [2, 3]

For now, out of necessity, our friends are buying drones from the United States and Israel, even while they move ahead with development of their own drones. [4]

The Neuron, a prototype for a European combat drone, has already been tested in France. The Neuron's design uses some elements of stealth technology to make it harder to detect. [5]

The British military is testing a drone named Taranis, which also uses stealth technology to evade detection. Taranis will have a considerable degree of autonomy. It will be able to avoid threats and identify targets on its own, without the need of a human controller. Fortunately, it will have to seek authorization from a human being before attacking a target. [6]

The degree of autonomy built into Taranis is probably a good idea, given that Britain lets fairly untrained operators fly its drones. Good onboard software would probably be more reliable than those operators, and as onboard computers become ever more powerful, the drone's ability to control itself will become more sophisticated and increasingly superior to even the best trained human operators. Even well–trained drone operators may not perform well because of boredom. Increasing drone autonomy is inevitable as a response to this problem. [7, 8]

The danger of fully autonomous, weaponized drones is obvious. Imagine the skies of the world filled with deadly flying machines, freed from human control, making their own decisions about which humans to eliminate. This is not a far–fetched idea. Simplified versions of such autonomous killing drones have already been tested. [9]

Calls for the international community to prevent the further development of such drones, as well as other types of "lethal autonomous robots," or LARs, have come from a United Nations official and from academics, political activists, and Nobel laureates. I think we can safely predict that nothing will come of these calls. Even if an agreement is reached, it will be ignored by military powers large and small. [10, 11]

Frontex, the pan-European border agency based in Warsaw, plans to perform surveillance beyond the borders of the European Union and to do so using drones produced in Europe. In cooperation with European drone manufacturers, this agency is calling for greater European drone capabilities. EU officials seem to be responsive to this call; expect a well–financed EU push into drone research and production. [12, 13, 14]

The European Union is working with an Israeli military contractor to develop drones that will be able not only to find vehicles — boats and cars — being used by criminals but will also be able to stop them dead in their tracks. The drones won't do this by firing missiles, but exactly how they will do it is classified. [15]

Turkey already produces its own unarmed drone, the Anka. Turkey has tried to buy armed Predator drones from the United States but has been repeatedly turned down. As a result, Turkey now intends to manufacture a version of the Anka with bigger engines to give the drone greater load capacity and to arm the new Anka with weaponry similar to that carried by America's Predator and Reaper drones. [16]

Iran has been developing its own drones and has apparently given some of them to groups such as Hezbollah to use against Israel. Iranian–built drones are known to have penetrated Israeli airspace. One of those drones possibly succeeded in surveying Israel's Dimona nuclear complex. At least one of the other drones was equipped with explosives, but it was shot down before it could do any damage. [17, 18]

Even countries without the technological and industrial ability to produce advanced drones of their own, or who simply prefer not to devote their resources to developing drones, can get around this problem by buying drones and the ground facilities to support them and training for the personnel who operate them. They can buy all of this from the United States. Countries doing exactly that range from the known and unobjectionable, such as South Korea, to ... Well, we don't know. That information is not available. We do know that the US government makes it easy for drone manufacturers to sell drones to those other countries, whoever they are. [19, 20]

The spreading use of drones has resulted in calls for them to be included in international arms treaties. Not only do drones cause injury and death to innocent people, says Medact, the global medical charity behind the call, in addition "[t]here is also some evidence that medical personnel and others who arrive at the scene to assist the injured have been targeted in drone attacks. This is a war crime." This is another call that will probably go nowhere. [21]

Drones don't have to be big and powerful or developed by the United States or some other drone power to be dangerous. Islamist terrorists in Germany devised a plot to assassinate people and possibly destroy buildings using ordinary model airplanes packed with powerful explosives. Fortunately, the police stopped them in time. [22]

A Drone in Every Corporation and Government Agency

In theory, there are limits to the use of drones in US airspace. In practice, these limits don't seem to be very effective. The Federal Aviation Administration (FAA) has to issue a license to operate a drone over the US at an altitude of more than 400 feet. It has been issuing those licenses speedily and by the hundreds to the US military, local law enforcement agencies, the border patrol, the FBI, state agencies, universities, and others. [23, 24, 25]

There's more to come:

> *The Federal Aviation Administration has been flooded with applications from police departments, universities and private corporations, all seeking to use drones that range from devices the size of a hummingbird to full-sized aircraft like those used by the U.S. military to target al Qaeda operatives in Pakistan and elsewhere.* [26]

Military drones are already in use all over the United States, and it's not just the military that's flying them. Thanks to a lawsuit filed by the Electronic Frontier Foundation, the FAA was forced to release records giving a glimpse of the numbers of such drone licenses and flights. It's a glimpse rather than a full view because some law enforcement agencies, including local sheriff's departments, refused to provide information about what type of drones they are flying, where they are flying them, and for what purpose. [27]

This is just the beginning.

The companies that manufacture military drones have been pushing to open our skies to tens of thousands of their products. As wealthy manufacturers never have any trouble doing, they have made a lot of friends in Congress. Sixty members of the United States House of Representatives are members of the House Unmanned Systems Caucus, also known as the Drone Caucus. These elected representatives of the people, just possibly influenced by the nearly $8 million in campaign contributions they've received from the drone manufacturers, are working hard to make the manufacturers' open–sky dream come true. [28]

At least they're working hard for someone.

In early 2012, their hard work paid off in the shape of the FAA Modernization and Reform Act, which requires the FAA to fully integrate drones into the national airspace by 2015. The FAA estimates that in less than 20 years, 30,000 drones will be sharing the skies with commercial airliners. [29]

Let's hope that by then, drones will be smart enough to be able to get out of the way of those airliners. Their current reliability is not encouraging. [30]

A Drone in Every Garage

What we've been talking about so far is the spread of powerful weaponized drones — the Reaper, for example. As we have seen, such drones have already spread beyond national armed forces and are now being used by internal police forces and paramilitaries.

What about the small drones, the ones that keep shrinking in size? Given that a lot of that development is already in the hands of private companies who want to sell their tiny drones to other companies or even to private individuals, it's clear that ever smaller drones will be proliferating rapidly and widely in the near future.

A great number of companies create high–tech products for the consumer market. Those products contain powerful, small electronic circuitry; powerful, small engines; and powerful, small sensors. Consumers are devouring those high–tech products, and so the manufacturers are buying large quantities of powerful, small electronic circuitry, etc. from their suppliers. This has driven rapid, ongoing development of such circuitry, engines, and sensors. They are becoming increasingly available and increasingly reliable, and their prices continue to drop. These are precisely the crucial components for creating ever smaller drones with ever greater abilities to spy and to collect, store, and transmit data.

Powerful drones are already available to consumers. A particularly impressive one is the AR.Drone, made by the French company Parrot. It's equipped with cameras, GPS sensors, an onboard computer, and Wi–Fi, so that you can control it with your iPhone or iPad or Android smartphone. You can use it to play war games with other AR.Drone owners. Or you can use it to spy on your neighbors. Parrot says that it has already sold over 500,000 of these drones. [31]

If you want one for yourself — purely for its entertainment value of course, not for neighbor–spying purposes — you can buy it online for just under $300. [32]

You might prefer to experiment with the cheaper, smaller, customizable Dragonfly drone. It starts at $100 and, as the name implies, it is the size of and looks like a very large insect. Future versions will be smaller and will have greater capabilities. [33]

Remember that you won't require an FAA license if your drone stays below 400 feet. Keep that in mind while you survey your neighborhood.

Perhaps you don't want to be limited by the product specifications of the Parrot or Dragonfly drone. Perhaps you'd like to create a drone whose hardware and software suit your needs, whatever those are. The world of non-governmental drones is moving in your direction. Google *open source drones* or *diy drones* and go exploring.

A lot of people are experimenting with modifying drones, and they're not all interested in spying on their neighbors. Some apparently want to shoot at their neighbors. Under FAA regulations, it is illegal to attach a weapon to your drone, but that has not stopped people from doing so — or at least claiming in YouTube videos to have done so. The desire to do this is clearly there, and it's not clear if the FAA can stop it. Thanks to the bizarre thinking of the rightwing majority on the United States Supreme Court, the Second Amendment could well now be interpreted to protect the right of individuals' drones to bear arms. We probably won't know until a privately owned drone shoots someone and the drone's owner is charged with a crime. [34]

Good Drones in the Air, on the Land, and in the Sea

Drones are not inherently evil. In fact, they are being used increasingly by corporations, governments, and private individuals in numerous clever and generally admirable ways. Scientists who work with drones see them as invaluable tools and would like to change the public's view of drones as primarily devices to spy and kill. [35]

Photographers are using them to take spectacular aerial photographs. Farmers are using them to inspect their crops. In Germany, the wind industry is using them to examine the blades on wind turbines, and the national railway company there is thinking of using drones to fight the problem of graffiti being sprayed on its property. The World Wildlife Fund plans to use drones to detect the poachers who have been killing elephants and rhinoceroses in Africa. Drones can go where humans can't, at least not safely. Swarms of drones might soon be used to transmit data from inside hurricanes, helping forecasters predict the storms' strength and trajectory. NASA is using drones to study volcanic plumes as part of a project to increase our understanding of the impact volcanoes have on the atmosphere. [36, 37, 38, 39]

Various research organizations are working on robotic snakes that will be able to slither into restricted places inaccessible to humans — for example, the rubble left after an earthquake, where the snakes could search for survivors (and not cause them to die of heart attacks, one hopes). Real progress on this front will probably be coming soon, thanks to the interest being shown in this technology by the US Army. Naturally, the Army is also interested in the use of robosnakes to perform surveillance and to detect explosives. [40]

Scientists from Stanford University are using a seagoing robot to track the movements of great white sharks and other sea creatures. The public can share the robot's experience on their smart phones or tablet computers. Many more such robots are planned. [41]

In Europe, a business–university consortium is testing an autonomous swimming robot shaped like a fish that propels itself by using the same motions as fish do. This robot is designed to search for pollution in the sea, such as chemicals that someone has illegally dumped, and immediately report the presence of such contamination. [42]

An even more ambitious robot fish has been created at the University of Singapore. This one also swims the same way that real fish do, but it has a greater ability to swim well below the surface. It is envisioned as having military applications but will also be used for underwater archeology, detecting leaks in pipelines, and laying underwater communication cables. It will operate autonomously. [43]

All of this will have a large economic impact. In addition to the jobs created at the companies manufacturing the drones, high–paying jobs are already opening up for drone pilots, and many more such jobs are expected in the future — perhaps as many as 70,000 in the next three years. [44, 45]

Clearly, not all drones are aerial. The term UAV is already an anachronism. We must learn to think in terms of robotic surveillance devices of increasing sophistication and with an increasing ability to live anywhere on the Earth, and under it, and in its oceans, as well as in our skies. For simplicity, however, we'll keep referring to all of them as drones.

Let's return to the sinister aspect of drones for a moment. Inspired by squids and octopi, the US military has developed a squishy little robot that can change its shape and camouflage itself while it crawls around. Expect to see far more of these "soft machines" in the future. Rather, expect not to see them. [46]

Talking about the sinister aspect of drones in a discussion of all the good things drones are doing is not cynicism. Any advance in the design and capabilities of good drones will be pounced upon by those intending to use drones for other purposes. Any of the "good drones" I listed above could be adapted for surveillance, spying, and even killing. And they will be.

Looking Ahead

We've seen where we've come from in the matter of drones and where we are now. Let's try to discern where we seem to be going.

Drones used for surveillance are getting smaller, moving toward insect size. The United States Air Force is already developing drones the size of insects that will mimic the appearance and behavior of insects. They will hide in plain sight. The plan is that these "bugbots" will be able to do more than gather intelligence. They will also be equipped to kill people. [47]

At the same time, drones can stay airborne for longer, fly farther, and gather more data. [48]

The appeal to people who want to spy on their neighbors is obvious.

It's also obvious that powerful information–gathering drones the size of insects will appeal enormously to law–enforcement organizations. Local police departments will like the idea of tracking bank robbers in real time, and they will adore the idea of spying on protestors demonstrating outside City Hall. Authorities at every level will leap at the chance to spy on people they consider threats, from peaceful political protestors to possible terrorists. The Internal Revenue Service will see an opportunity to monitor potential tax cheats even before they file their returns.

Drone manufacturers are very aware of these huge and lucrative markets. One manufacturer's Web site goes into considerable detail about the use of its drone for investigating crimes, controlling traffic, and controlling crowds. [49]

Two ongoing internal wars, the War on Drugs and the War on Terror, have resulted in the dismantling of our civil rights. At the same time, and not coincidentally, those two wars have seen the transformation of our police departments into paramilitary organizations, equipped with the most powerful weapons the Department of Defense is willing to pass on to them.

Drones developed for military use will inevitably join the arsenal of military weapons in the hands of local police departments.

At first, there might be some restrictions in place. Perhaps police will be provided with versions of the drones that lack weapons. Inevitably, that will change. It's likely that the first type of weapon added will be disruptive and supposedly non–lethal weapons for crowd control or for control of individuals (for example, in hostage situations). The widespread, indiscriminate use of Tasers, resulting in numerous deaths, is a foreshadowing of what we can expect once weapons are added to crowd–control drones. [50]

Worldwide, most people disapprove of US drone strikes. Americans, on the other hand, approve strongly of US drone strikes executed in other countries against people deemed a threat to America. "Other countries" is the important part. Americans would probably also be opposed to drone strikes if they were happening within the USA — if you never knew, for example, when your favorite Starbucks might be blown up by a missile fired from a drone because a suspected enemy of the government was believed to be inside and without regard for whether you and other innocent people were also in there, sipping overpriced lattes. [51, 52]

We're not there yet, but as I said, we will soon be seeing domestic drones equipped with non–lethal weapons. Coming soon to the skies near you will be police and federal drones equipped with rubber bullets, bean bags, Tasers, and the ability to destroy personal computers and other electronic equipment by emitting electromagnetic pulses, or EMPs — powerful bursts of electromagnetic radiation. [53, 54]

Domestic use of such non–lethal drones will probably meet with public approval. Inevitably, the non–lethal weapons will be replaced — perhaps slowly, incrementally — with deadly ones. Will the American public accept this changeover? As long as they're afraid of domestic criminals and foreign terrorists lurking around every corner, many Americans will.

For some time now, drones have been used by law–enforcement agencies in the US and other countries to spot marijuana plants from the air. Drones are quite effective in this role. [55]

(The US is also using drones to detect drug trafficking on land and sea, although this effort seems to involve both technical and political difficulties. [56, 57])

This use of drones is very good, from the point of view of the people waging our absurd and socially destructive War on Drugs, but it also has frustrating limitations. Identifying marijuana plants from the air is straightforward. Identifying what's inside cargo being loaded on a truck is a different matter. Is the cargo legal, or is it a drug shipment? Our current drones can't see inside the containers to find out. Law enforcement needs and very much wants drones the size of small insects — spying machines that no one will notice but that can infiltrate a suspected drug trafficking operation, take a tiny sample of a suspected shipment, test it on the spot, and send back enough information to enable the drug warriors to get the needed warrants and send in the human enforcers.

But even that would solve only half the problem. The other half is knowing *where* to send those powerful insect–

sized drones. How will law enforcement know where the drug trafficking is taking place?

In TV cop shows, informers make life easy for the drug-warrior heroes by passing word to them about where the evil deal is going down. Informants play a part in real-life police work, but actual law enforcement has always largely depended on the painstaking accumulation and analysis of data from a variety of sources.

In recent years, the amount of that data has exploded.

Much of this explosion is due to the growth in electronic eavesdropping. Telephone calls and e-mails are intercepted and their contents stored for future analysis. Your cell phone constantly reports your location, and that information, constituting a record of your movements, is stored. Information gathered by the American Civil Liberties Union shows that hundreds of police departments across the country routinely monitor and collect such cell-phone data, almost always without the legally required warrant. [58]

Drones and surveillance cameras, combined with increasingly sophisticated facial recognition software, also provide a record of your daily life.

Corporations are also gathering huge and growing amounts of information about private citizens, and this data is being increasingly passed on to government agencies.

In the past, such great quantities of data would have been useless precisely because of their quantity. Filtering, collating, and analyzing the data would have been done by human beings, and they would have been overwhelmed.

Now it's no longer necessary to use humans for those tasks. Instead, it's all done by advanced software running on powerful computers. As a result, this vast amount of data has become a vital tool of law enforcement. It can be used not only to track the activities and movements of individuals in remarkable detail but even to predict their future behavior.

As we'll discuss in **Section 2: Diminishing Privacy**, this data gathering is driving the development of ever smaller and more powerful drones. The ideal information-gathering drone of the near future will be the size of a small insect, indistinguishable from real insects, able to stay in the air for extended periods, and cheap enough to be turned out in huge numbers to ensure that no potentially important conversation is overlooked, no matter where it takes place.

It won't be practical to have human operators controlling individual drones, once they number in the millions. At best, human operators will provide general oversight to swarms of drones. Individual drones will have to be autonomous — independently controlled by extremely small but extremely powerful computers contained within the drones.

Swarms of millions or tens of millions or hundreds of millions of drones disguised as insects will fill in the surveillance gaps that current drones and surveillance cameras are subject to — i.e., the places that the eyes of current drones and surveillance cameras cannot see. They will also lead to the inevitable next step in law enforcement: the targeting and elimination of individuals.

Suppose a heavily armed man has taken hostages and is holed up with them in a house so well barricaded that police can't attack without fear of killing the hostages. If an insect drone were small enough to get inside the house, and if it were sufficiently intelligent to find the hostage taker inside the house, then it would only need to contain a fairly small amount of explosive. It could land on the top of the hostage taker's head and detonate itself, simultaneously signaling the police that the threat had been eliminated.

I don't think most of us would object to that. After all, 70% of Americans currently approve of using drones to kill suspected terrorists abroad, and 49% approve of killing US citizens living abroad who are suspected of being a terrorist threat to the United States. Surely even more would approve of using a tiny drone to eliminate a dangerous man openly threatening innocent hostages, no matter where the drama was taking place. [59]

But why wait for someone to take hostages? What if the police are absolutely convinced that someone is a threat to public safety, or perhaps just to the safety of police officers? That could be due to the person's actual, observed behavior, or it could be due to what the predictive software mentioned above thinks he's likely to do.

As the use of predictive software spreads, both local law–enforcement agencies and national–security organizations at the Federal level will be creating their own very long lists of people whose deaths would, in the view of those organizations, make the nation safer.

Elimination by insect drone of an armed man holding hostages will surely be popular. High-quality video taken by the drone and broadcast to the police, right up to the moment of detonation, will probably be shown repeatedly on the evening news and will accumulate millions of hits on YouTube. Assassination of people who might possibly pose a threat at some point in the future will be a different matter. The authorities responsible for those deaths will be well advised to make them look like accidents or natural deaths. That's hard to do when you blow someone's head up.

I hope this is not too optimistic a view of the public's reaction to such domestic assassinations. We might some day reach the point where no disguise will be necessary and extra-judicial assassinations within America will be performed openly. Fortunately, we're not there yet.

But how much does public approval matter? Drone technology is advancing more rapidly than our democracy is devolving. We are probably only a few years away from the day when a drone disguised as a mosquito verifies the identity of a public-safety or national-security threat, lands on his exposed skin, injects a minute amount of a deadly poison into him, and immediately flies away. The target thinks he's been bitten by a mosquito and forgets about it. A few hours later, he dies of an apparent heart attack. By that time, the poison had broken down into substances normally found in the blood. No one but the people behind the assassination will know that it was not a natural death.

The easier it gets to do this, the more often it is bound to happen.

We've been talking about the future of the use of drones by government agencies. The world's corporations will not be far behind.

Corporate information requirements differ from government ones. Rather than predicting who will endanger public safety or national security, corporations need to know what their competitors are planning and what new products they're developing. Autonomous drones disguised as insects will carry industrial espionage to a new level.

I don't think that corporations will be interested in carrying out assassinations disguised as heart attacks. It's more likely that they'll use the proprietary information their tiny drones gather to recruit and hire away a competitor's best people or to steal trade secrets. They might also use personal information for blackmail, but that's a risky avenue that could expose the blackmailing corporation to legal repercussions.

In the long run, what's probably more important than corporate drones is the ongoing merger between corporate and government databases. That's already happening. The result is that privacy is steadily disappearing. The details of our lives are increasingly visible to the prying eyes of government agencies and powerful corporations.

As we have already seen, numerous organizations other than the military are using drones — for example, police forces, border control agencies, scientific organizations, news organizations, search and rescue agencies, and environmentalists. We have also seen that increasingly cheaper, smaller, and more powerful drones are available to the general public.

This is part of a general trend, one that will continue and even accelerate. The drones available to civilians will continue to get more powerful, cheaper, and smaller. Remember that no license is required for a drone that operates below 400 feet altitude. No one will know how many drones are operating in the air just above us, especially as the drones get smaller and harder to see, or harder to distinguish from insects.

Thanks to the existence of the Internet and the spread of access to the Internet by means of WiFi and the cell-phone network, the ability of drones to gather large amounts of data and transmit it to a home base via the Internet will accelerate. That home base no longer has to be a corporate or government office. It can be literally someone's home and a desktop or laptop or tablet computer in that home. It can even be a smart phone.

Thus, information about you, even very private information about your activities and videos of your private life, will be contained in databases stored not just in government repositories but also on the hard drive of your neighbor's computer. Software that can analyze that data and draw inferences or predict future behavior will become available to everyone. The versions used by private citizens may not be as powerful as the software used by government agencies and private corporations to sift through their huge databases, but it won't have to be. It will be sufficient to satisfy someone's curiosity about you and even to deduce aspects of your behavior that you'd much rather not have anyone know — for example, whether you're cheating on your wife or your taxes.

Insects at War

Before 10 years have passed, the air above our heads will be filled with innumerable gnat–sized flying drones, indistinguishable from real insects — except that Raid won't work on them. They'll be ubiquitous. They will record sound and video. Some will be able to eavesdrop on electronic communications. The only protection against them will be carefully constructed airtight rooms with shielding against radio signals, something most of us won't have access to.

Electronic countermeasures will become common. You'll install devices in your home to interfere with the internal electronics of the gnat–sized drones. That will work until a new generation of drones appears whose inner workings are based on optical circuitry.

Once that happens, the only defense against the gnats will be other gnats — gnat–sized hunter–killer drones that will be able to tell which gnat is an insect and which one is a drone and that will be equipped to destroy the latter kind.

Why would this even be necessary? Because the tiny drones filling the air around us won't all belong to the American government or American corporations. Many of them, perhaps most of them, will be from elsewhere — from foreign governments, foreign corporations, and no doubt from terrorist groups. [60]

At some point, sabotage gnats will appear. Think of them as suicide bomber gnats. The explosive power of such a gnat would be insignificant if used against, say a building, although a large swarm of such gnats, detonating simultaneously, could do some damage. They will be more useful in attacks on sensitive equipment, such as computers.

Gnat–sized drones designed for sabotage or assassination will have to operate in various locations, especially inside buildings, where communications with their home base will be unreliable or impossible. They will only be able to complete their missions if they contain a considerable amount of computer power and artificial intelligence. They will have to be able to operate autonomously. We'll discuss this further in **Section 4: Diminishing Computers**, but for now, contemplate the fact that the tiny drones filling the air around us in the near future will increasingly be able to find their targets by themselves and initiate action against those targets based on their own judgment.

Below the level of human senses, a war will be underway.

Currently, we hear much about cyberwar, a war consisting of software attacks launched against computers. We see on the news that computers in Iranian nuclear research installations have been attacked by software "worms." These reports are accompanied by much speculation in the press as to who created those worms, with the United States and Israel being the chief suspects. We are told that China's Red Army is mounting a powerful, continuous, and intensifying cyber attack on American and European government, corporate, and military computers.

The coming war between insect–sized drones will be different. We won't hear anything about it. We'll think that we're living in a world at peace. The press will be as unaware of the war as the rest of us. But this war will be waged fiercely, from the ground level to high up in the air. The stakes in this war will be very high indeed — as high as they were during the two world wars and the Cold War. If one country wins this simultaneously minuscule and immense war, it will rule the world.

But it's more likely that there will be no winner. As tiny drones become both cheaper and more powerful, governments all over the world will be turning them out in vast numbers. The factories will become smaller and more widespread, and they will be protected against sabotage gnats by their own swarms of hunter–killer gnats.

The drones will keep getting smaller, cheaper, and more numerous. The defensive measures will become more ingenious and complex.

The war won't be between two sides, two huge alliances, like the two world wars and the Cold War. It will be a war of many sides, with each combatant under constant attack from all of the other combatants and launching counterattacks against all of them. Indeed, most of the time it won't be possible for any country to know for sure which other country is attacking it, and so it will launch its killer and sabotage drones at everyone else. In the end, this war will devolve into the equivalent of World War One's trench warfare — grinding, horrendously costly, and seemingly endless.

Political Consequences

In the meantime, we private citizens will be going on about our lives unaware of this war. We'll be aware only of the increasing defense budget and our decreasing privacy and freedoms. We'll be aware of the occasionally successful act of sabotage without knowing that it's part of a war. We'll also be aware of the disturbingly frequent deaths of political leaders here and abroad, the results of targeted assassinations by drones that got through the defenses mounted by hunter–killer drones.

At some point in this process, probably fairly early on, drones owned by individuals will become useless. They will be seen as a threat because they will provide dangerous information to civilians and because they will also allow civilians to communicate too freely with each other. These privately owned drones will be sitting ducks for the vast swarms of hunter–killer gnats operated by governments and by corporations under contract to governments. Private citizens won't be able to compete technologically on this level, at least not if they try to do so as individuals.

Our political system won't be able to handle this. Decades of continual war have already leached the strength and conviction from our democracy. The public's commitment to America's founding ideals has proven to be weak indeed in the face of the perceived threat of terrorism. In addition, a cynical security–state apparatus — virtually a second, secret government — has played upon the public's fear and cowardice to dramatically expand its power and to gravely weaken civil liberties. Soon, that secret government will have extraordinarily detailed information about every citizen and the ability to eliminate anyone who is thought to be a threat to its growing control.

The diminishing size and growing numbers and capabilities of drones will be paralleled by the dwindling influence of democratic government and the growing power and control of the shadowy security–state apparatus.

This shadow government is not entirely governmental and hasn't been for a long time. The line between government and industry has always blurred during wartime. Decades of perpetual war have eroded that line almost into meaninglessness. (Valerie Plame Wilson, the American spy whose identity was treacherously revealed by Dick Cheney, and her husband, Joe Wilson, a former US ambassador, have referred to one part of this as "a vast intelligence-industrial complex that is largely unaccountable to its citizens." [61]) This is particularly true for the giant corporations that produce our government's weapons — including drones.

Variations on this theme are proceeding in other countries, as well.

A sham democracy will continue in the United States and some other countries, but it will increasingly be a façade. True power will be vested in corporations and security agencies in the West and in bureaucratic hands in China, but the difference between the two will be meaningless. Under this scenario, the citizen will be powerless.

However, as we will see, the technology that is giving governments and corporations such frightening power over us will also, in time, provide us with a powerful defense.

A Bad Summer for Insects

Something bit John's neck. He cursed and slapped. The insect evaded his hand and flew away with an angry buzz.

"The bugs are awful this year," John said. "They're everywhere."

"I know," Mary said. "They're not even waiting till evening."

She looked at the tables set up in their back yard, the grill on the patio, and the cooler filled with beer and soft drinks. "Everything's ready. People will be arriving soon. I'll turn on the bug zappers."

"Kill those little bastards," John said.

"Calm down," Mary said. "Have a beer."

"Where's Elmo? He's better than any bug zapper."

"Probably hiding under the bed. He can tell there'll be a lot of people here."

"Some watchdog."

Their friends started arriving. The yard filled up with people stuffing barbecued meats down their throats, guzzling beer and soft drinks, and talking too loudly. Mostly, they talked about how bad the bugs were this summer.

Henry came over carrying a paper plate loaded with ribs covered with barbecue sauce in one hand and a half-empty beer in the other. He sat down at the table across from John. "This is the worst summer for bugs I've ever seen," he said.

"Mary's got bug zappers going all over the yard."

"Yeah, I saw. I think the insects have evolved, or something. I haven't heard any of them getting zapped."

"Great. Evolved insects. That's just what we need." John had finished eating a while ago. Now he was concentrating on drinking. He had his fourth beer in his left hand. With his right, he pointed at a fly that was circling over Henry's head, a few feet up, just out of reach. "I think he's got an eye on your food."

Henry looked up. "He's been following me around. So far, he's keeping his distance." He looked around, making sure that no one was nearby. He lowered his voice. "Let's talk about that work."

"He's determined," John said, looking up at the fly, which was still hovering about Henry's head.

"He can give up. He's not getting his feet in my barbecue. Where's that dog of yours? He's better than any bug zapper."

"Hiding from all the people, probably."

Henry had been hiding a DVD under his paper plate. He looked around again and then handed it to John. "That's everything you need." He lowered his voice. "There's a file called Materials. Go to Home Depot and buy all of that stuff. It's what I'll need to do the work in your house. There's a folder called Henry. All the data is in there for you to redo my books for me."

"Speak normally. There's no one around aside from your buddy, the fly."

"Hey, it's Elmo!"

The big golden retriever had emerged from the house. He was standing near one end of the table, his eyes fixed on the fly. He was glaring at the insect. Elmo hated flies.

Elmo bounded onto the table. Henry snatched his plate of food out of the way. Elmo leaped into the air. The fly buzzed away but not quickly enough. Elmo's jaws snapped shut on the insect while the dog was still in mid air. He landed on the concrete beyond the table, chewed a couple of times, and swallowed.

The two men cheered and thumped Elmo on the back. Elmo looked pleased with himself.

"Now I can eat in peace," Henry said.

"Let's go inside," John said. "I want to make sure I can read those files."

They left. Behind them, Elmo looked startled. He whined. He jumped in the air. He turned in rapid circles. Then he shot through the startled crowd on the lawn and disappeared into the bushes along the back fence.

It was cold in John's office. "I cranked the AC up to compensate for everyone going in and out and holding the back door open," John said.

Two flies buzzed past Henry's head. "What the hell is this?" Henry said. "The cold air doesn't even bother them!"

"It's like they're a new breed of fly this year," John said. "They get through screens and they don't care how cold it is inside. I bet they'll be around during the winter, too."

The two men tried to ignore the flies hovering above them and concentrated on John's computer monitor. The discussed the files on Henry's DVD, their barter arrangement, and the way John would need to do the taxes for Henry's business in order to eliminate any traces of their arrangement and Henry's other barter deals. Unconsciously, even though they were quite alone, they spoke in hushed tones. That was silly and pointless, of course.

* * * * *

Bad news came in three pieces the next day.

Hours after all the party guests had gone home, when John was locking up the house for the night, Elmo was nowhere to be seen. He didn't respond to John's repeated calls.

"I guess he wants to spend the night outside," John told Mary.

"He's sulking," Mary said. "He's angry at us because of all the people we had here today."

But the next afternoon, when she was picking up trash from the party that she had missed in the fading light of the previous evening, she found Elmo hidden in the bushes at the back. He was dead. Blood was caked on his lips, which were drawn back from his teeth. Blood had run from his eyes and ears and dried on his face. Oddly enough, although there were flies buzzing overhead, none of them seemed interested in Elmo. She called the city and was told to put the dog's body in a plastic yard bag and leave it by the curb for pickup.

She told John when he came home from work in the evening. By then, Elmo's body was gone.

"He must have been out in the street during the night," John said. "Got hit by a car and crawled into the back of the yard and died there."

"I thought you'd be more upset."

"Normally I would be, but I've got something else on my mind. I got a call from the IRS today. They know all about the deal I've got with Henry — the things I do with his taxes, the work he does on our house in exchange. They even know about Henry's other barter deals. I don't know how they found out."

"Oh, John! Are you going to go to jail?"

"They threatened me with that. I made a deal with them. Henry's a much bigger fish than I am. He does a lot of shady stuff with his construction company. They're going to leave me alone in return for me telling them everything I know."

"So Henry will go to jail?"

"It's him or me."

"Then it should be him," Mary said. "And we'll be okay?"

"Yes. I swear to you, I'm never stepping off the straight and narrow again. They scared the hell out of me. I'm going to play strictly by the rules for the rest of my life."

Above them, a couple of flies were walking across the ceiling.

2
DIMINISHING PRIVACY

A Tsunami of Data

In **Section 1: Diminishing Drones**, we talked about the growing flood of data about private citizens being gathered by corporations and government agencies and how useful that data is to those gathering it. In this section, we'll look at some specific examples of the data and how it is used, and we'll discuss further the implications this growing flood of data has for privacy and the further development of surveillance drones.

A sort of feedback cycle has come into existence. The very usefulness of the flood of data creates a desire on the part of the data gatherers for ever more data. The tsunami grows larger. The usefulness increases accordingly. The cycle continues.

Some agencies in our own government seem to feel that we have no right to hide our personal data from them. Our data is automatically theirs, and they don't even need a search warrant to get it. Documents obtained by the American Civil Liberties Union have revealed that the Department of Justice and the FBI feel that they don't need a search warrant to review Americans' e-mails, Facebook chats, Twitter direct messages, and other private files. The IRS feels the same way. The FBI is in the habit of issuing National Security Letters: documents that require the organizations receiving them to turn over their customers' personal data, e-mail records, phone records, etc. No warrant has to be issued beforehand by a judge, and almost all National Security letters include a gag order forbidding the recipient from telling anyone that such a letter has been received or what it concerns. Hundreds of thousands of these pernicious letters have been delivered. The courts, which should be protecting us from such abuses, are not doing so. When the FBI sent 19 National Security Letters to Google demanding customers' confidential data, Google refused to comply, insisting that the demands were illegal without a warrant. A federal district court judge ordered Google to comply with the letters and hand over the data. [62, 63]

Google objected, but other corporations don't seem to be so punctilious about the Constitution. AT&T and other Internet service providers have been cooperating happily with the feds, letting them eavesdrop on our telephone calls and other communications. The only thing that the companies wanted in return was legal protection, given that they could have been prosecuted for breaking federal wiretapping laws. The Justice Department has taken care of that problem by arranging legal immunity for the companies. [64]

This legal immunity will become the rule, not the exception, if a proposed law known as CISPA, for Cyber Intelligence Sharing and Protection Act, ever passes. CISPA would give blanket approval to the sharing of Internet traffic information between corporations and the government. Among the corporations pushing for this law are our friends at Microsoft, Facebook, AT&T, IBM, and Apple. Fortunately, thanks to the work of various civil liberties and Internet privacy organizations, CISPA has been blocked. Powerful forces will keep working to push it through, however. Possibly by the time you are reading this, CISPA will have become law.

Without the help of CISPA, issuing those National Security Letters must be so tedious for the FBI, such an encumbrance! It would be so much easier if the feds could eavesdrop directly whenever they wanted to on all of that juicy Internet traffic, all that delectable private data. That must be why the FBI is pushing for new laws that will give them that sort of easy access. The proposed laws would force social networking Web sites such as Facebook, Google, and Skype to add back doors to their systems — i.e., technology that would permit easy electronic access for the FBI. The sites would be fined heavily if they did not comply. [65]

The FBI has been using technology that allows it to track individual cell phones for the last 20 years. The device used, called a stingray, collects data from cell phones belonging to innocent bystanders, not just from the one belonging to the individual the FBI is particularly interested in tracking. Civil liberties groups have opposed the use of stingrays for this reason. The American Civil Liberties Union went to court to challenge the use of the device in one particular case because "[b]y failing to apprise the magistrate that it intended to use a stingray, what the device is, and how it works, it prevented the judge from exercising his constitutional function of ensuring that warrants are not overly intrusive and all aspects of the search are supported by probable cause." The judge hearing the case ruled against the ACLU and in favor of the FBI. This case has set a dangerous precedent for the future use of such surveillance technology. [66]

Dutch police will soon be given the authority to hack into computers in Holland or elsewhere. They will be allowed to install spyware, read e-mails, and delete files. Ostensibly, the primary reason for these new powers will be the fight against terrorism and child pornography. Only a fool would believe that the exercise of these powers will be limited to those two areas. [67]

Fearing that terrorists are now more technologically advanced than the government agencies investigating them, the British government is pushing for new surveillance laws that would require communications firms to collect and store data about almost everything done online by everyone in Britain. The records would include not only telephone calls but also what Web sites people click on and whom they chat with on social networks. Opponents of the proposed laws fear that if Britain succeeds in implementing them, Western countries that have so far resisted this response to terrorism will follow suit. [68]

Thanks to the huge amount of data they are collecting, law enforcement agencies at every level, in the US and elsewhere, can track the activities of individuals with an accuracy and degree of detail that the governments of even the worst dictatorships in history could only dream of.

It is important to understand that the people who are the targets of surveillance and data collection are not known criminals. They are not even people who have done something that makes them look like potential criminals. Everyone is a target. We are all considered potential criminals.

Moreover, this has been going on for a long time. As revealed recently by William Binney, a whistleblower who resigned from the National Security Agency (NSA), that agency has been intercepting electronic communications from all Americans for many years and storing those communications in immense databases. [69, 70]

The NSA is not alone.

The New York City police department has amassed a database of cell phone telephone call logs, mostly the calls to and from stolen cell phones, but including other cell phones. (These are logs — who called the cell phone or was called by it, when, and for how long — and not the actual content of the calls.) The database does not contain only calls made or received by cell phone thieves but also those made or received by innocent citizens. [71]

This is not limited to New York City. Federal and local law-enforcement agencies have subpoenaed millions of cell-phone records from cell-phone companies. The data delivered by the cell-phone companies in response to these subpoenas include records of cell-phone calls by millions of people not suspected of involvement in any crimes. You could say that they are collateral damage.

Nonetheless, their information is now stored forever in law–enforcement databases. [72]

The State of Maryland has established a network of Automatic License Plate Readers (ALPRs) around the state, a network that is constantly being expanded. These are all linked to a centralized database. As the number of ALPRs increases, the movements of more and more vehicles are being tracked and their movements recorded in the database. The records will remain in the database permanently. [73]

This technology is spreading quickly. Maryland was the pioneer, but police departments everywhere in the US have installed ALPRs of their own and are permanently storing records of people's movements by car and truck. Once again, these are records of the movements and activities of perfectly ordinary citizens who have done nothing illegal and in almost all cases will never do anything illegal. Something similar happened in the United Kingdom a few years ago. Despite public opposition, the result was a nationwide database of vehicle movements. The creation of an identical, nationwide database in the US appears to be inevitable. [74]

Governments adore this stuff. The appeal to repressive governments is obvious, but democratic governments are snapping it up, too. A company named Gamma Group has been selling surveillance software called FinSpy to law–enforcement and intelligence agencies in 25 different countries, including some extremely repressive ones. FinSpy invades computers, including home computers. It bypasses antivirus software. Once it has installed itself,

FinSpy can record everything you do on your computer, including what keys you strike on your keyboard. It can copy files from your hard drive and send them to Gamma Group's servers. [75]

For years, the National Security Agency has been collecting and examining e-mail messages and telephone calls — billions of them. Now it is building an immense data center in Utah to make the task of handling all of that data easier. The data center will contain enormous computing power. Moreover, the NSA has come up with a technique for cracking encryption. This new technique, combined with the computing power at the Utah data center, will give the NSA the ability to read intercepted e-mails from corporations and foreign governments, despite the sophisticated encryption methods used to keep such e-mails secure. Of particular interest to the NSA is the ability to read e-mails containing financial information, stock transactions, business deals, and diplomatic and military secrets. [76]

Corporations and government agencies use extremely sophisticated encryption methods, far more sophisticated than the level of encryption available to the ordinary citizen who wants to keep the contents of his private e-mails safe from prying eyes. Given that the NSA can now break those highly sophisticated methods of encryption, it's clear that communications between ordinary individuals will be an open book to the snoops in Utah.

You're not always on your computer, of course, and not all of your communications with other people are done by e-mail. There are times when you're far away from your computer — riding the bus, for example.

You may be aware that a lot of buses are equipped with video cameras. They're there to deter crime. In other words, when you are riding the bus, the bus is watching you. Increasingly, it's also listening to you. Across the United States, buses are being equipped not only with surveillance cameras, but also with hidden microphones to record every conversation that takes place aboard them. Much of the cost of installing and operating this spy equipment is being borne by the Federal government, in particular the Department of Homeland Security. All of the words spoken on buses, polite or impolite, innocent or not, will eventually end up yet another collection of enormous databases. [77]

The many databases we've been talking about are proliferating and becoming ever larger, so plans must be made to accommodate this growth. Perhaps just as important, the databases must be integrated with each other so that connections can be made between items of data in different databases. A few words spoken here, an item bought in a hardware store there, a book glanced through in a bookstore, a car trip taken to a place the driver doesn't normally visit — it must be easy to correlate all of these and infer disloyalty, no matter how shaky the logic behind the correlation may be. We are all in those databases, and the pictures of us that they allow to be drawn become increasingly complete. Suspicions of disloyalty or untrustworthiness, no matter how baseless, will be increasingly common. We'll all be living in the world of Franz Kafka's nightmares.

The FBI is planning a billion–dollar upgrade to its existing and already huge fingerprint database. The new database, Next Generation Integration, will contain fingerprint records, of course, but it will also contain iris scans, photographs that can be searched using facial recognition software, palm prints, measurements of gait (how you walk), voice recordings, and descriptions of scars and tattoos. Other law–enforcement agencies will have access to this database. Civil libertarians fear that the database will quickly grow to include information about millions of innocent citizens, such as their photographs, fed into the database by the growing network of public and private surveillance cameras. [78]

Facial recognition software is becoming remarkably accurate and ever more widely used, by corporations as well as government agencies. Moreover, the corporate and government databases containing such software are becoming increasingly connected. The number of cameras connected to these databases is growing rapidly. The identities and movements of people who pass by those cameras are recorded permanently. New rules put in place by the Obama Administration allow far greater use of such data by Federal security agencies. Internal regulations previously in place, intended to protect citizens' privacy to some degree, have been jettisoned. The presumption of innocence, going back to ancient Rome at least, has been jettisoned along with those rules. We are all now presumed guilty. If some day you cross a line you didn't know existed, a line that was drawn in some secret conference room, the evidence that will convict and sentence you is already being collected and recorded. [79, 80, 81]

The courageous defenders of liberty and privacy who pack the halls of Congress are apparently not going to be of much help. They may like to give speeches about how much they love the Constitution, but they love to vote for increased government surveillance of ordinary citizens.

Using the powers granted to the government by the Foreign Intelligence Surveillance Act (FISA), the Bush administration listened to private telephone calls and read private e-mails without warrants and with the enthusiastic cooperation of US telecommunications companies. FISA includes immunity for those telecommunications companies. You can't sue them for helping the government to spy on you. FISA was due to expire in 2012, but Congress passed and President Obama signed a bill extending it to 2017. Don't place any bets on the law being allowed to die a well deserved death then. [82]

Don't bet on public outrage putting a stop to the spread of spying on us, either. Americans have always paid loud lip service to freedom, and we regularly proclaim our dedication to it, but in reality we Americans see the world as a terrifying place, and we are desperate to be protected. Giving up our privacy is a price we are all too willing to pay. One week after the April 15, 2013 Boston Marathon bombings, a *New York Times*/CBS News poll found that 78% of respondents favored installing video surveillance cameras in public places. Similar poll results, showing a willingness to sacrifice freedom in return for security, are common after terrorist attacks. The number of people who expect more terrorist attacks also rises after each such attack. Americans are behaving as other people have throughout history. Governments have always been adept at inducing fear of an outside enemy in order to garner support for repressive laws. [83]

The spy apparatus, spying on other countries and spying on us, has grown immensely since the September 11, 2001 terrorist attacks. A two–year investigation by *The Washington Post* found that "no one knows how much money it costs, how many people it employs, how many programs exist within it or exactly how many agencies do the same work." The bureaucratic machine uncovered by the *Post* is of astonishing size and complexity. From the point of view of our individual freedom and privacy, we can at least be thankful that the investigation also discovered that the machine contains much redundancy and incompetence. Those same two failings are not comforting, however, when one realizes that that machine is also responsible for detecting and protecting us from actual terrorist threats. In any case, the machine is here to stay, and it continues to grow rapidly. [84]

Coming Soon to a Spy Camera Near You

The increase in the power of surveillance hardware and software is remarkable. So is what it might be able to do in the future.

Most of us are aware of the growing numbers of surveillance cameras of various sorts. They're not only increasing in number. They are also becoming increasingly powerful — able to take pictures of ever greater resolution and under conditions that, not long ago, would have made photography impossible. Even greater advances in camera capability are coming. Scientists at Nanyang Technological University in China have developed a sensor that will allow cameras to take clear pictures at light levels of one-thousandth the level now required. The new sensor also requires one-tenth as much electrical power as current camera sensors. [85]

Even walls might not protect you from spy cameras in the not-too-distant future.

Engineers at the California Institute of Technology have created microchips that could eventually make it possible for smart phones to take pictures through walls. In the near future, these chips will become extremely valuable in medicine, letting doctors peer some distance into the body without subjecting the patient to the damage caused by X-rays. They will also be extremely useful in homeland security, making it possible to quickly detect weapons hidden inside innocuous-looking objects such as stuffed toys. Rapid development of this technology is inevitable. Will it actually reach the point where surveillance cameras can watch you through the walls of your home? It's too soon to say, but if that does prove to be technically possible, then we should assume that it will happen. [86]

A different approach taken by engineers at University College London (UCL) has already reached the see-through-walls stage. All they require is the signal from a WiFi router or hotspot, and those are present almost everywhere in modern cities. When you move through a room where such a signal is present, your motion creates changes in the signal (the Doppler effect). The UCL engineers built equipment that detects these changes and constructs an image of the body that caused the change. The more WiFi signals there are, the more accurate the picture of the objects on the other side of the wall. Predictably, one organization that has expressed great interest in the UCL work is the British Ministry of Defence. [87]

Or perhaps spy agencies won't bother with such fancy technology. Instead, they'll sneak software onto your smartphone that will use the phone's camera to surreptitiously transmit photographs of your surroundings. The Naval Warfare Surface Center and Indiana University's School of Informatics and Computing collaborated on such software to see how much information about the phone's surroundings could be gleaned from photographs taken at random intervals. The answer is, a great deal. They concluded that it should be possible not only to construct a detailed three-dimensional model of the phone's surroundings, but even to read financial documents and personal information on the computer monitor the phone's owner is looking at. [88]

The public was made aware of the growing capability of facial recognition software when it was used to identify the prime suspects in the Boston Marathon bombing in April 2013. Tamerlan and Dzhokhar Tsarnaev, the two brothers who are believed to have planted the explosives, were initially nothing more than blurred faces in surveillance videos and cell phone photographs. Scientists at Carnegie Mellon University's CyLab Biometrics Center used software to sharpen the images and rotate the faces so that they were facing the viewer. The face of one of the brothers was then successfully matched to a face in a database. The same team is working on extending the distance at which cameras can take pictures that facial recognition software can use to successfully identify people. So far, they have extended that distance to 60 feet. [89]

You probably remember the scandal about the new airport scanners that were a little bit too effective. They showed Homeland Security employees what people walking through the machines looked like underneath their clothing. The public reaction was sufficiently loud and outraged that those scanners were abandoned.

But Homeland Security isn't really interested in what you look like naked. They would rather know if there are traces of drugs or gunpowder on your clothing or body. They would like to know the level of adrenaline in your blood (because of the assumption that someone planning a terrorist attack has more adrenaline pumping through his system than the average person). New scanners that will soon be installed will tell Homeland Security all of the above, and what you had for breakfast as well. These new gadgets are fairly small, extremely sensitive, and extraordinarily quick. You won't have to walk through a special archway to be inspected by them. You won't even know that you're being inspected by them. And they probably won't be limited to airports for very long; eventually, they'll be installed everywhere. [90]

Keeping track of what people are doing now is just the start. Computer software is already being used to predict future criminal behavior. For now, it's being applied to people who have been convicted of crimes. The idea is to determine whether such an individual should be granted parole from prison, and if so, under what conditions. Raytheon has developed somewhat similar predictive software that deals with more general behavior — that is, it's not limited to known criminals. Given the databases mentioned above, it is inevitable that further developments of this software will be applied to the data that describes all of us. [91, 92]

You may think your record is spotless. Software that analyzes your entire recorded history may well disagree. It will flag you for observation. Eventually, it may flag you for more than observation.

Facial recognition software is part of a more general field known as *biometrics*, the science of identifying individuals by physical characteristics or behavior. It is already remarkably accurate and will become far more so. Combine this with the vast databases mentioned above, and it's clear that law enforcement will soon be able to find you wherever you are whenever it wants to.

Rather, it will be able to do so if it has up–to–the–minute images of you, such as from surveillance cameras or drones.

Now, that represents a problem.

Even in the United Kingdom, often called "the most surveilled" of industrialized Western countries thanks to the ubiquitousness of CCTV (Closed Circuit TV) surveillance cameras, it's still possible to find places where you can't be seen. That's true despite the fact that the UK is a geographically small and densely populated country.

In geographically large countries with great areas of open space, such as the United States, Canada, Australia, or Russia, surveillance is considerably more difficult. Huge areas of those countries are not covered by existing surveillance equipment. To track the movement of people in those areas, and in the parts of cities where the surveillance–camera eye currently doesn't see, law–enforcement software used to rely on satellites and airplanes and now relies increasingly on drones.

Remarkable though today's drones are as devices to gather information and kill people, they are still limited. For example, if you're in a thick forest, with trees sheltering you from the open skies, they can't see what you're doing in great detail without making themselves visible to you. Even if you're in the city, they can't tell what magazine you're reading in the privacy of your bathroom — not yet, anyway. [93]

Clearly, the solution is for drones to become much smaller and much more numerous. Ideally, as we've already discussed, they would be the size of small insects, and we, the subjects of their spying, would pay no more attention to them than we do to insects. Such drones are not here yet, despite repeated Internet rumors. But they are getting close. [94, 95, 96]

However, there would still be places where you could not be watched. With care, even drones the size of gnats could be excluded from some places. To circumvent this problem, drones will have to get smaller still.

And they will.

3
DIMINISHING COMMUNICATIONS

One of the characteristics of the 19th and 20th centuries was the growth and development of communications. As the European colonial empires and the United States and Canada grew to immense size, they bound their widespread settlements together with the telegraph, then the telephone, and eventually radio.

In time, the telephone became common in ordinary homes. Cell phones and other mobile devices have made communication portable. The Internet and e-mail have made communication even more convenient. We can make videos and post them on Web sites for the world to see. We take it for granted that we can speak to the people we know almost whenever we want to and almost wherever we are. In democracies, we like to think that we can talk to our friends by phone about any subject at all. We can criticize the government or our bosses or other friends. We assume that no one is eavesdropping. Even in democracies, this is naïve.

Throttling the Web

People who don't live in democracies are not subject to this misconception. They know how dangerous it can be to speak their minds. At the same time, they also see communication devices and the Internet as tools to spread information damaging to the regime and as weapons to possibly undermine and overthrow it.

Naturally, repressive regimes respond to this threat by eavesdropping on communications and by doing their best to control access to the Internet.

China no longer allows anonymity on the Internet; users must be known by their real names. Authorities can delete posts or Web pages because of content. Even giant corporations have trouble fighting the Chinese government. Google recently tried to help Chinese users of its search engine by warning them when they were treading on dangerous ground. Under pressure from the Chinese government, Google gave up and dropped the warning. According to some reports, the Chinese government has found ways to limit what is returned by searches. Worse is coming. China is now creating its own next–generation Internet. When it's in place, personal computers, servers, and other devices will only be able to connect to the Internet if they have prior approval from the government; non–approved devices will be completely shut off. [97, 98, 99, 100]

Iran has a population of 75 million people, and half of them have Internet connectivity. "Social media" sites, such as Facebook and Twitter, are very popular there — and, in the eyes of the government, very dangerous. The Iranian government is developing software that will let it control how much access its citizens have to those sites. It is also creating an internal network, a national Internet, which will replace the worldwide Internet the rest of us use and which it hopes will keep its citizens satisfied while providing much more government control. In the meantime, while this national Internet is not yet up and running, the government has blocked its citizens from accessing Gmail and Google's search engine. Even more dangerous to the government than Facebook and Twitter are foreign news sites, such as the BBC and CNN. Iranians have devised ways to access these sites, circumventing the government's attempts to block them. The government has responded by blocking these circumvention methods. For Iranians, the cyberwall separating them from the outside world continues to grow and to be harder to penetrate. [101, 102, 103]

The government of Pakistan, becoming ever more oppressively Islamic, has blocked access to Facebook and YouTube. The autocratic government of Tajikistan has ordered Internet service providers to block a large number of Web sites, including Twitter and many Russian-language sites. Ethiopia has blocked access to Internet technologies that permit anonymous communication. Anyone using Skype can be sent to jail for up to 15 years. People can also be imprisoned for using various social media sites. [104, 105, 106]

Saudi Arabia has cut off its citizens' access to the encrypted free telephone and text messaging service Viber.

This came after Viber refused the Saudi government's demand that it allow the government to monitor the messages carried by Viber. The same demand has been delivered to Skype and Whatsapp, which also provide Saudi citizens with unfettered communication with people outside the country. [107]

On a different tack, the government of Pakistan shut down cell phone service in at least 15 cities during protests led by Islamic activists. The government said that this was to prevent terrorists from using cell phones to detonate bombs remotely, but many Pakistanis believe that the government was really trying to shut down the protests by keeping the organizers from communicating with each other. [108]

In Russia, the Internet spread far and wide while the government wasn't paying attention. Indications are, however, that Vladimir Putin wants to make up for lost time and "protect" Russians from dangerous Western influences transmitted via the Internet. No one knows yet how the Kremlin plans to accomplish this, but Russians fear that dangerous bloggers, for example, will be imprisoned and that more and more Web sites will be blocked. An existing Russian law, ostensibly designed to fight child pornography, is already being used by the Kremlin to force Web sites, including major ones such as Facebook, to remove content that has nothing to do with child pornography. The removed content is not political; it was deemed objectionable for various non–political reasons. [109, 110]

Singapore is more subtle about repression than those countries, and it is taking a more subtle approach to controlling the news. Online news sites now have to obtain a government license and post an expensive performance bond. This puts them on a par with newspapers and television stations, which have long been subject to the same rule. The difference is that online news sites are the only truly independent news sites in Singapore, and they have been instrumental in the ability of the government's political opposition to reach voters. [111]

Such wretched things don't happen here in the West, of course. Or so we like to think. And yet, very much like what happened in Pakistan, cell phone communications were blocked in rapid transit stations in San Francisco in an attempt to forestall demonstrations over a shooting by transit police. [112]

Right now, in the United States, control over the Internet is largely in the hands of a few huge corporations, such as Comcast, Verizon, and Time Warner. Their interests aren't political, but financial. They want to keep their existing control because the Internet is a money-making dynamo for them. As a result, they work to make sure that alternative free access to the Internet either doesn't exist or is kept to a minimum. [113, 114]

As long as this is the case, the government doesn't need to assert direct control over the Internet in order to prevent dangerous activities. Even without using its drones to spy on people, the government can rely on the giant communication companies to provide it with the needed data. The government rewards those corporations by not regulating them, including turning a blind eye to their anti–competition actions. It's a cozy relationship of mutual back–scratching.

There are some barriers to this cooperation in the form of laws and technical barriers preventing smooth sharing of data. But those who disapprove of the public having unfettered online freedom of expression can take heart. There is a mechanism in the works to deal with these problems — CISPA, the Cyber Intelligence Sharing and Protection Act, which we discussed in **Section 2: Diminishing Privacy**. Inevitably, those behind this bill say that it is needed in order to protect the United States from cyber threats. Just as inevitably, in practice it will serve mainly to intimidate citizens and interfere with the free exchange of information. Supporters of privacy have so far managed to keep it from becoming law, but its backers have not given up. They have a good chance of succeeding eventually. [115, 116]

It's not just governments that fear the Internet and the wider, outside world it brings with it. There are closed religious communities everywhere, including in the United States, that keep their members emotionally and intellectually trapped by cutting them off from knowledge of and access to the outside world. In the past, that meant keeping out worldly newspapers and books. That was relatively easy. The advent of the Internet has created serious problems for them. They can try to prevent Internet access through computers, which is difficult but not impossible, but they can't prevent members of the community from accessing the Internet through smartphones. The result is inevitable. For Hasidic (ultra–orthodox) Jews trying to extricate themselves from their stifling, crippling little world, the Internet has been, you could say, a Godsend. [117]

Drones As WiFi Hotspots

An interesting way for protestors to maintain communications with each other during a demonstration was suggested by an organization named Tomorrow's Thoughts Today. The group has created small drones that can act as WiFi hotspots. These could fly above the demonstrators and provide an alternative way to connect to the Internet if authorities cut off normal access. [118]

However, even this clever idea, or any other kind of alternate Internet access provided to protestors by people sympathetic with their goals, can't really protect against the government shutting down communications.

The Internet, the channel through which so much of our communications travel, is remarkably robust. Although the common belief that the Internet and its predecessor, ARPANET, were designed to survive a nuclear attack is not true, it is nonetheless the case that the network can handle a lot of hardware failure and other outages and still keep functioning. This is a result of its highly distributed design, heavily redundant pathways between servers, and the packet–switching method used to send information across it. [119]

And yet, as we've seen, governments have managed to shut off access to the Internet locally and even nationwide. This does not require great ingenuity or technical wizardry on their part. There are a number of choke points within the interconnecting network of servers that constitute the Internet — places where the flow of data can be stopped. Some of this is an accidental byproduct of the design of the Internet. However, increasingly, choke points are being deliberately designed into the system by government fiat or because of corporate wishes. [120, 121, 122]

Even those flying robot WiFi hotspots can't get around this problem. Your text message to your fellow protestor a block away can go from your smartphone to the little robot circling overhead, but from there it goes to a server at an Internet provider, and then it must pass through a chain of servers and back to another circling robot and down to your friend's smartphone. Along the way, it has to pass through some of those choke points. If the government and its corporate friends have control over a sufficient number of those choke points, or just over the most important ones, then that text message will never reach your friend's phone, or it will do so in a garbled and unintelligible form.

Clearly, what's needed is some way for the hovering robots to pass messages directly between each other and thus avoid those choke points entirely.

Enter peer–to–peer, or P2P, networking. In P2P networks, the devices connected to the network don't depend on centralized servers to handle specific tasks. Instead, each device can, for example, receive a message and pass it along to another device on the network. [123]

In practice, in many P2P networks, the Internet is still used as the pathway between the devices. If you want to set up P2P communication between your computer and the computers of friends scattered across the United States, the most practical way for your computers to all connect to each other is by means of the Internet. You wouldn't want to pay for thousands of miles of dedicated optical fiber as an alternative. Truly direct connections between your computer and those of your friends would only be practical if you were all living very close to each other, preferably in the same apartment.

Various types of P2P communication have become extremely popular as a way to exchange, for example, music and video files. Since the goal is to exchange files and not to avoid government snooping, these P2P networks all use the Internet as the medium of exchange. The result is that these P2P file exchanges now constitute a large part of the data moving across the Internet — large enough to create a serious capacity problem. That in turn has led the giant corporations that handle most Internet traffic, such as Comcast, to block or limit the amount of P2P traffic they will allow on their part of the network.

The warfare has been escalating. P2P networks have adopted various techniques, generally referred to as *protocol obfuscation*, to disguise what they are sending across the Internet and to prevent Comcast and the gang from picking P2P traffic out from the rest. These techniques are not foolproof. There are still ways to detect P2P traffic on a network. P2P communication therefore remains vulnerable to attack from those who want to limit it or stop it completely. [124]

However, it is possible to create a P2P network that avoids using the Internet entirely. With the right software, devices such as the hovering robot WiFi hotspots can quickly set up what's known as a *wireless ad hoc network* among themselves. This is a highly flexible arrangement that allows new devices to join the network quickly and participate in forwarding messages. The devices communicate directly with each other by means of WiFi. The devices themselves control and configure the network; no system administrator is required. The network is adaptable and dynamic; if one of the devices in the network is disabled — for example, deliberately shot out of the air — the network immediately reconfigures itself so that it continues to operate properly. Similarly, it can easily add new devices without being disrupted. [125, 126]

Each device in such a network requires a fair amount of computer power, but we have already reached the technological point where sufficient power can be packed into a physically small device. At the time this was written, researchers were devising ways to create wireless *ad hoc* networks between smart phones. [127, 128, 129]

Even if wireless *ad hoc* networks connecting smart phones don't come about, the helicopter drone WiFi hotspots we were discussing earlier would be quite a bit larger than the typical smart phone and would therefore contain sufficient computer power to be part of an *ad hoc* wireless network. In the near future, as we will discuss in **Section 4: Diminishing Computers**, even the gnat–sized drones we talked about **Section 1: Diminishing Drones** will have more than enough computer power onboard to become part of such a network.

In other words, those private robot drones circling above a crowd of protestors will be able to keep the demonstrators in contact with each other. The only way law enforcement would be able to shut down that communication would be by shooting down all of the robots.

The Coming Age of Communication

Now let's look a bit further into the future.

The desire to communicate with each other is natural for human beings. We are, after all, social animals. When repressive regimes try to thwart this desire, they are tackling a powerful drive that is innate in all of us, and people have always enlisted the latest technology to fight that repression.

During World War Two, Britain used radio stations to broadcast messages intended to give heart to the repressed populations in Nazi–occupied Europe. During the Cold War, the United States did the same with the populations of the Soviet Union. The USSR obviously considered these broadcasts a threat to its control. It responded by broadcasting static on the frequencies used by the US broadcasters, Radio Free Europe, and the Voice of America.

Body:

In the Soviet Union, writings that the regime wanted to suppress were printed and distributed from one reader to another. In some cases, rebels were forced to use typewriters and produce carbon copies. However cumbersome the means, forbidden literature was reproduced and distributed. These copies were known as *samizdat.* [130]

When the Shah of Iran tried to maintain his grip on his country and prevent a revolution by exiling the leader of the religiously based uprising, Ayatollah Khomeini, Khomeini responded by recording his speeches and lectures on cassette tape, many copies of which were then smuggled into the country and distributed widely. Those tapes played a major role in the uprising that toppled the Shah, causing one of the revolutionaries to say that "tape cassettes are stronger than fighter planes." [131]

Now imagine those WiFi hotspot robots we talked about earlier reduced to insect size and produced in great numbers. This is similar to what we talked about in **Section 1: Diminishing Drones**, but now we're talking about gnat-sized drones that are not designed to spy or perhaps assassinate but rather to provide free electronic communication to people everywhere — communication that cannot be shut down by repressive governments or by giant corporations.

All it would take for this to come about is the ability to pack sufficient computer power into a very small space.

The historic trend for computer chips has been toward decreasing size and increasing power. The numbers illustrating the trend in size and power never fail to

astonish. The chip in the birthday card that sings "Happy Birthday" to you when you open it contains more computing power than the combined computers of the Allied forces at the end of World War Two. The typical cell phone of today contains more computing power than existed in all of NASA at the time of the first moon landing. At the same time, the cost to produce these chips and the amount the consumer pays to buy them keep going down. In fact, some are questioning whether computer manufacturers will be able to continue to make a profit. [132, 133]

Eventually, there will be major changes in the fundamental way computer chips work. Breakthroughs in physics and engineering will change the very meaning of the word "computer." But even without such revolutionary changes, the trends we are seeing in computer chips now — decreasing size and cost, increasing power — mean that those insect-sized drones we've been talking about will be getting ever more powerful and ever more numerous.

I mentioned that the cost to produce chips keeps decreasing. However, that applies to the cost per chip, not to the cost of the factories in which the chips are made. Those facilities are already enormously expensive and are getting more so. This means that while private citizens will be increasingly able to build increasingly capable drones for themselves, they won't be able to build the tiny, powerful microchips that will make the drones powerful tools for surveillance and communication. We'll talk about this again in **Section 4: Diminishing Computers**, where we'll see why this should not be a barrier to the continuing evolution of tiny, extremely capable drones in private hands.

As we saw in **Section 1: Diminishing Drones**, individuals can already buy fairly small drones. As more people become interested in flying their own drones for amusement or to spy on their neighbors, the drones available to the public will become smaller and cheaper.

No doubt some people will be interested in creating their own small drones. They will find it increasingly easy to do so.

They can buy suitable power sources. Extremely small electric motors — some of them smaller than a dime — powered by small batteries and costing only a few dollars apiece are already commercially available. [134]

Electric motors available to the public will probably keep getting smaller and more powerful. How small can they get? The smallest electric motor ever made is the size of a single molecule. Of course, you won't be buying that one anytime soon. [135]

So you can buy the tiny motor and the tiny battery, but building a flying robot insect is not a trivial matter. Fortunately, very soon, it will be quite easy, thanks to the advent of the revolutionary technology known as 3D printing, or additive manufacturing.

In 3D printing, a machine called a printer (some of them resemble the ink–jet printers used with home computers) builds the desired object out of layers of liquid, powder, or sheets of various types of polymer. The printer follows a blueprint, called a template, which tells it how to build each layer of the object it is creating. Thus the same printer can be used to create many different objects, depending on which template it is given.

3D printing is being used increasingly in industry, but the printers are also being bought by ordinary people. Small, home versions of the printers are now available, and the prices are falling. The current status of such printers has been likened to the early days of personal computers. The price for a home 3D printer has now fallen below $1,000. [136]

Templates for building many different objects by means of 3D printing are now available on the Web. In the comfort and privacy of your home, you can now print items ranging from musical instruments to powerful guns. [137]

This technology has already been used to create a small drone. Robotics engineers at Cornell University used 3D printing technology to build the whole device, including the moving parts. They used a commercially available small electric motor and batteries. The resulting drone weighs less than four grams and is able to lift the motor and batteries into the air and hover for 85 seconds. [138]

That may not sound like much, but this is just the beginning. We can expect rapid improvements in the design, lifting power, and flight duration of these small drones. We can also expect that drone hobbyists will be able to download templates for small drones from the Internet and feed those into their home 3D printers.

This will lead to proliferating numbers of small drones that can function as WiFi hotspots, passing messages securely between themselves without using the Internet.

These drones will constitute a people's Internet, free and public, completely decentralized, accessible via cell phone, laptop computer, tablet computer, and any other WiFi-equipped device.

As the encryption methods programmed into these drones improve and the number of them increases, eavesdropping on this people's Internet will become increasingly difficult. Even the NSA won't be able to decrypt these messages if it can't physically intercept them, and it won't be able to intercept them if the drones passing the messages between each other are physically close together. The most practical way to eavesdrop, and perhaps disrupt the network, will be with great numbers of equally small and powerful drones released by government authorities and corporations.

One defense against such attacks will be still greater numbers of people's Internet drones communicating over very short distances, perhaps even physically touching, in order to pass on messages.

As the hardware improves, the increasing data storage capacity of the drones will make it increasingly feasible for the drones to store great amounts of message data and pass it on to other drones in quick bursts during physical contact. This will make interference very difficult. Enforcement drones will have to make physical contact with virtually every drone that's part of the public Internet in order to be sure of intercepting every message. That's not an impossible task, but it is a truly daunting one, and it would mean that the air around us would be so thick with enforcement drones that visibility would be close to zero all over the world. This dense cloud of enforcement drones would interfere with other forms of communication, such as the regular cell-phone network. It would also play havoc with satellite surveillance.

This public Internet will not be a very high-speed Internet, but it will be secure, and it will be spread increasingly widely over the world. Borders will mean nothing to this network. Government regulations and proscriptions will be irrelevant to it.

Practically anyone, anywhere will be able to talk to anyone else anywhere. They will also be able to exchange files with each other — text files, video files, data of all kinds that governments don't want people sending to each other across borders or even within borders.

Everyone an Eavesdropper

We've been talking about the public Internet as a ubiquitous and secure communication channel. But it's important to understand that the drones making up this Internet will also be the most powerful and widespread eavesdropping system in history.

In addition to growing storage capacity, drones will carry increasingly sophisticated video and sound equipment. Fewer and fewer places will be safe from their prying eyes and ears. Government and corporate wrongdoers will have to resort to doing their work in increasingly sophisticated sealed rooms. Those without access to such safe places will quickly see themselves on television screens everywhere, with the public watching them saying and doing things they thought were private.

Citizens will use drones to catch politicians betraying the public trust. Governments will use drones to spy on each other. Corporations will use drones to steal secrets from rival corporations. The smaller, more powerful, and more numerous drones become, the more intrusive this spying will be.

Of course this eavesdropping won't be limited to corporate and government employees. Private citizens will be horrified to find their most private activities showing up on YouTube.

Attacking the Public Internet

With governments of all kinds, including the most nominally free ones, devoting increasing resources to intercepting communications, the public Internet will be seen as a threat.

Many governments will outlaw drones made by ordinary citizens. People creating and releasing their own drones will laugh at those laws.

Governments will be forced to take the war to the next level. If the public Internet can't be penetrated and controlled, it will have to be destroyed. That means destroying the huge and increasing numbers of drones that will constitute the public Internet.

The safest way to do that without also damaging or destroying desirable infrastructure, such as the commercial cell phone network, will be to produce tiny drones designed to identify undesirable drones and destroy them.

"Undesirable" won't only mean the insect–sized WiFi hot spots. Government and corporate drones will be sent out in great numbers to find and destroy the spy and attack drones of other governments and corporations. This warfare will probably be invisible to the naked eye, but we will be aware of its effects if the attack drones are able to hamper the public Internet significantly.

Even though the drones will be tiny, their offensive weapons will be impressive, with steadily growing power. Of course, governments and big corporations will always have the edge in this battle. How are citizens to respond? How will they preserve the public Internet's role as a subversive communications network and a tool for uncovering official wrongdoing?

The only practical answer is for public drones to keep getting much smaller and much more numerous while simultaneously getting better at communicating and storing data and at eavesdropping. The future of this particular war isn't ever bigger and more destructive weapons but rather ever smaller, harder to detect, and ubiquitous ones.

How small can they get? Quite small, indeed, as we'll see in **Section 4: Diminishing Computers**.

I Didn't See Anything about It Online

John was upset when he came home.

"This guy at work, Harry, he said he heard that there was this protest in Idaho that turned really violent. The troops fired on the protestors. A bunch of people were killed."

"Idaho?" Mary asked, not really paying attention.

"Yeah, Idaho. Harry said there was some kind of big protest over a mine or a pipeline or something like that. The government sent in troops, and they shot a bunch of the demonstrators."

"I was watching the news just before you got home," Mary said. "They didn't say anything about it. Where did he hear this?"

"Oh, I don't know. He always claims to be hearing stuff like this. Harry's kind of weird. He has friends who were involved, I think. Anyway, he said that there were going to be big sympathy marches all over the country because of what happened. There'll be one here, too. It sounded like it could get bad here, too. I'm going to see what I can find online."

"Good idea," Mary said.

John sat down in front of the computer they shared, set on a small table in a corner of the kitchen, and began looking at the Web sites he relied on for non–local news. A half hour later, he stood up. "Nothing," he said. He still looked worried. "Maybe I should call a couple of the local TV stations and see if they know anything."

"Maybe you should just forget about it," Mary said. "It's not a good idea to draw attention to yourself after that trouble you had with the IRS."

"You're right. Anyway, since I couldn't find anything at all about it, it probably didn't happen. Maybe one of Harry's friends was playing a joke on him. I'll tell him that tomorrow."

But John never did get the chance to do that, because when he got to work the next day, he learned that Harry had not shown up, and someone claiming to be a relative of his had phoned in his resignation.

4
DIMINISHING COMPUTERS

You may have heard the claim that we went to the moon with a slide rule — i.e., that engineers working on the Apollo project used slide rules to perform their calculations, or that the astronauts flying on the missions carried slide rules and used them to determine how to land on the moon.

This is nonsense. Those calculations were done with computers. On the ground, some of the most powerful computers then available were used, and on the Apollo spacecraft, the astronauts used specially designed and programmed onboard computers.

Yet it is true that both the ground and onboard computers of the Apollo project, impressive as they were to those of us who worked on that magnificent undertaking, were puny compared to today's typical desktop or laptop or tablet computer, or even to a modern smart phone.

We've all seen the comparisons between what were once considered powerful computers and the kinds of devices that are now common in every household. The great difference in computer power between then and now is something that most people take for granted, but for those of us who worked on those old machines, the numbers can still be a source of astonishment.

The Apollo Lunar Module, or LEM, was the part of the spacecraft that landed on the moon. (Officially, it was the LM, but the acronym LEM stuck to it. That was from the original name, the Lunar Excursion Module, because in the early design, the vehicle was supposed to be able to move about somewhat on the lunar surface.) The two astronauts in the LEM depended on the spacecraft's onboard computer, the Apollo Guidance Computer or AGC, for the landing and even more for the launch from the lunar surface, the return to lunar orbit, and the rendezvous with the Command Module, which would take them back home to Earth.

Your desktop computer probably has at least four gigabytes — four billion bytes — of random access memory, or RAM. The AGC had one kilobyte — one thousand bytes — of RAM. Your computer's Central Processor Unit, or CPU, probably operates at around two or three Gigaherz (two or three million cycles per second). The AGC's CPU operated at 1 Megaherz — one thousand cycles per second. On your computer, you might have one terabyte — one trillion bytes — of space to store data on your hard drive. The AGC didn't have a hard drive. Instead, it had read–only memory, or ROM — twelve thousand bytes of it. Yes, it was enough to send men to the moon and bring them back from it, but it took some of the finest minds in 1960s computer engineering to figure out how to cram the necessary programming and data into that tiny computer, and how to design it in the first place.

We engineers on the ground were not subject to the size and weight limits that applied to what was crammed into the LEM. When I worked on the Apollo project at NASA's Manned Spaceflight Center (later renamed the Johnson Space Center) in Houston, I used a Univac 1108 computer. This stupendously fast behemoth cost over one million dollars, and it was worth every penny. Its CPU was a bit faster than that of the AGC, and it probably had around one megabyte of ram — one thousand times as much as the AGC. There was no hard drive. Storage consisted of as many punch cards as you could handle.

During the early 1970s, at Martin Marietta Aerospace, I worked on the unmanned Viking Mars lander project. I performed software development and data analysis on a CDC 6500 computer, a multimillion-dollar monster that was ideal for scientific programming. It was blazingly fast and could read in punchcards at a tremendous rate. That also meant that when something went wrong during the card-reading process, it could chew up a huge number of punchcards at record speed before frantic humans could stop it, but never mind that: We were living in the future!

Still later, in the 1980s, the transition to desktop computers began. I was working at an oil and gas software company when one of my fellow programmers was the first in the group to be upgraded to a personal computer that contained its own hard drive. A five-megabyte hard drive! Five million bytes! We crammed into his cubicle to watch the slowly blinking red hard-drive light in awe. "Five megabytes!" we all said, in wonder. "Man! You'll *never* fill that up!"

The smart phone sitting on my desk as I type this has a 1000 megaherz processor and two gigabytes of storage, expandable to 32 gigabytes. Of course, it also has a digital camera and various apps, and it can access the Web via WiFi or the cell phone network — none of which existed during the dark ages described in the previous paragraphs.

We used to be very aware of the continuing flood of technological wonders. Now the technological flood is just the way the world works. We are no longer surprised at the rapid pace of increasing computer power being packed into ever smaller, lighter packages. We expect any computer we buy to be eclipsed in a matter of months, if not weeks.

This general trend is sometimes characterized as "Moore's Law," after an observation made by Gerald Moore in 1965. He noted that the number of transistors on an integrated circuit had been doubling every year. Later, he changed this to every two years. Nowadays, his law is usually quoted as specifying a doubling every 18 months.

This isn't a law in the same sense as Newton's Laws of Motion or manmade laws. Rather, it's an observation of a technical trend. However, the trend that Moore pointed out has held remarkably steady in the almost 50 years since he made it, despite frequent predictions that electronic miniaturization would soon reach an inevitable limit and that Moore's Law was about to be repealed by Mother Nature. Moore himself predicted that the trend could not last beyond the year 2020 or 2025, because by then transistors would be around the size of a single atom.

That has actually happened already, at least in the laboratory.

Researchers at North Carolina State University have developed a method for making semiconductor films one atom thick. The films can be produced on a large scale. [139]

Scientists at the University of New South Wales in Australia have created a fully working transistor that consists of a single phosphorus atom. They were not the first to do this, but they were the first to do it by means of a process that could be used to manufacture computer chips containing such tiny transistors in an industrial setting. [140]

Such a transistor would be very tiny indeed. A phosphorus atom has a diameter of 196 picometers, or 196 trillionths of a meter. By contrast, the smallest transistors used in Apple's popular and powerful iPhone smart phone and iPad tablet computer are about 32 nanometers across, or 32 billionths of a meter. So the smallest transistor in an iPhone is about 163 times as big as the phosphorus–atom transistor created at the University of New South Wales.

There will be many obstacles to surmount before the general public can buy electronic devices containing transistors of this tiny size. This will happen, though, and when it does, the effect on computers will be revolutionary. In particular, quantum computing, a field now in its infancy, will blossom. Quantum computers will be enormously powerful tools for scientists and engineers, enabling them to quickly solve problems in their fields that can't be practically solved with the kinds of computers we have now. [141]

From the perspective of everyone else, computers will become vastly more powerful. We'll be able to do everything we do with them now, but much faster, without worrying about limitations in memory size, and we'll pay much less for those very powerful machines.

Even the definition of the word *computer* will change as computer electronics become increasingly integrated into everything from household objects to clothing, and in time into our bodies. And all of these things with computers built into them will be able to communicate with each other and over the Internet.

This will be in large part a result of the rapidly diminishing size of transistors, but it's more accurate to say that it will happen as the result of the diminishing size of computer microchips.

At the heart of a computer or smart phone is a microchip, or integrated circuit. This is a collection of transistors and other electronic components built on a layer of material, usually silicon or germanium. This complex circuitry is designed and programmed to perform numerous computer functions. Strip away the power supply and all circuitry the computer uses to communicate with its monitor, keyboard, mouse, etc., and what you're left with is pretty much the microchip. That is the basic computer.

Modern microchips are quite small, but they contain billions of transistors. As we all know from using our modern computers and smart phones, microchips are very powerful devices.

Apple's iPhone, which is really a powerful, small computer, is built around a tiny microchip, the Apple A6, which is a square of about 10 millimeters on a side. The more powerful iPad tablet computer is built around a modified version of the same chip, called the Apple A6X, which is about 11 millimeters on a side. As I mentioned above, the smallest transistors in both versions of this microchip are 32 nanometers across, or 163 times the size of the single–atom transistor created at the University of New South Wales.

Now imagine that all of the transistors in the iPhone microchip could be replaced by such single–atom transistors. For the sake of simplicity, let's assume that all of the other components of the microchip could also be reduced in size by the same amount. (This is not an unreasonable assumption. The shrinking size of transistors has been accompanied by a similar reduction in the size of other electronic components.) That powerful iPhone microchip would be reduced to a square of about 60 micrometers — 60 millionths of a meter — on a side. That's just over half the size of the largest particles found in windblown dust. [142]

Or, to look at it another way, a tiny object the size of a speck of dust blowing in the wind could contain the power of an iPhone and still have almost half of its volume available for other uses.

We'll refer to these dust–sized computerized devices as motes. Because of the material it would be made of, such a mote would weigh about as much as a speck of dust of the same size. Dust is a world traveler. It's constantly being carried by the wind from one continent to another. The computerized motes we're talking about would behave the same way. They wouldn't travel as far as the smallest dust particles. The larger the particle, the less time it spends aloft before drifting down to the ground. Once on the ground, it can be rolled along the surface by the breeze or lofted up again by a stronger wind. Inevitably, our dust motes will get smaller as the technology advances. Future versions will stay up for longer. Eventually, any such mote will traverse the world. [143]

The one–atom transistor is in the future. For that matter, it may turn out that it's impossible to move it from the lab and into industrial production. So the iPhone microchip reduced to half the size of a mote of dust may not happen. But we may not need transistors that tiny in order to have powerful computers the size of motes of dust.

More than two years ago, scientists in Taiwan created a powerful microchip that is only nine nanometers — nine billionths of a meter — across. This microchip is designed to be a memory chip rather than the sort of microchip on which computers and smart phones are based. However, once the technology used to create it is adopted by the microchip industry, it will be applicable to the production of microchips of all kinds. [144]

The new Taiwanese microchip is about one seven thousandth the size of the hypothetical shrunken version of the iPhone microchip we were talking about earlier. It wouldn't be as powerful as the iPhone microchip, but a mote of dust could contain many thousands of them and still have plenty of room left over for other miniaturized devices.

You're not likely to be building these microchips, or even much simpler and larger microchips, in your garage. Perhaps there will be a dramatic technological breakthrough in the future that will make that possible, but no such breakthrough is now in sight. The factories used to produce microchips — semiconductor fabrication plants, or *fabs* — contain technologically highly advanced equipment. At the heart of the fab is the clean room, which must be free of even the smallest speck of dust. Clean rooms are constructed so as to keep vibrations down to an extremely low level. The temperature and humidity within the clean room must also be tightly controlled. The cost of building and equipping such a fab can be as high as $10 billion. [145]

Microchips are in remarkably widespread use, and they're on their way to becoming ubiquitous. They're in our computers and our smartphones and all our other electronic gadgets, of course, but they're also embedded inside our pets, so that we can be contacted if the animals are found wandering far from home. Microchips are embedded in consumer products to simplify stocking in warehouses and to help supermarkets keep track of their inventory. They are embedded in so–called "smart" running shoes so that the shoe can adjust to the wearer's weight and running style. There are microchips in fishing reels, supposedly to improve the user's cast. You can buy toilets containing microchips that turn off the water in case the toilet leaks or overflows. One such toilet can monitor your health by evaluating your urine; it will then send that data to your doctor's office. Microchips are found in tombstones. They can be activated by a smartphone, and they respond by transmitting videos about the dead person to the smartphone. [146]

This is equivalent to saying that a wide range of microchips are already available to people who want to integrate them into homemade drones. That will apply to the microscopic ones, as well, once those become commonplace.

Of course, the software built into these microchips isn't designed to operate such drones. The chip hardware is powerful, but if the chip is to fly a drone, then the software needs to be replaced. Fortunately, commercial products are already available that will let you do exactly that. [147]

Power Supply

Obviously, our dust motes will need a power supply. Surprisingly, there are quite a few options on the horizon for this.

A team of researchers from Harvard University and the University of Illinois have used 3D printing technology to produce lithium–ion microbatteries the size of a grain of sand. These batteries would be somewhat too large for our dust motes, but this development is just a first step. Even smaller batteries are inevitable. [148]

The drawback to using batteries for the dust motes is the need to recharge them. Some special-purpose motes might be designed to operate until their batteries are drained and then go permanently inert, but in general, that would scarcely be practical. Motes will need some way to generate or obtain power to keep their batteries charged.

Ongoing improvements in photovoltaic cells — the basic elements of solar electric arrays — might make it possible to power the motes with solar energy. This power source would only be available while the mote was exposed to light, of course. At other times, the mote would have to rely on battery power. Long dark periods would therefore present a problem. For example, in motes operating at night in areas where there were no manmade lights, their batteries might be drained before morning.

A mote traveling on the wind could generate electricity for its own use by interacting with the Earth's magnetic field. When a wire moves through a magnetic field, an electrical current is created in the wire. This is the basic principle used to generate electricity. The same principle would generate an electric current in a microscopic wire inside a dust mote as the mote moved through the Earth's magnetic field. The Earth's magnetic field is very weak, and the wire would be tiny, so the generated current would be extremely small. However, the motes would not require much electricity to operate. The generated current would probably be sufficient. But it would be very unreliable. Any motes that drifted into a dead air space, a place where there is no air movement at all, or motes that became stuck in the rough surface of a static object, would have to rely on battery power. Once that ran out, the motes would be dead unless by chance they started moving again.

A much likelier power source for the dust motes, and a very reliable one, is the manmade energy bathing all of us all the time — for example, microwave transmissions, radio and television broadcasts, and WiFi networks. The idea that this ambient energy could be captured and used to power small electronic devices has been around for a while. Thanks to recent research, it will soon be practical. Tiny batteries, recharged as needed from this power source, will probably be included in the motes for backup. By the time the first of our computerized dust motes set off on the wind, they will have more than enough power to do their work. [149]

Sound and Video

As mentioned above, the dust motes we are envisioning will have room inside them for more than powerful computers. Among the devices most likely to be packed inside are sound and video recorders.

The video recorders won't be the kind we are used to using, however. Some things can't be shrunk down to dust–mote size, at least not using technology we now have or can currently foresee. It's not just a matter of miniaturizing the recording equipment. Nature itself limits what that equipment can record.

At this point, the state of the art in camera miniaturization seems to be a camera created at Cornell University that fits on the head of a pin. [150]

This camera is an impressive technological achievement, but it doesn't take pictures that any of us would e–mail to friends and family. Because of its tiny size, the Cornell camera is only a 20–pixel camera. By contrast, the new Apple iPhone 5 smartphone has an 8–megapixel (eight million pixels) camera, and the new Samsung Galaxy S4 Zoom smartphone has a 16–megapixel (16 million pixels) camera.

Think of a pixel as a way to describe one of the many tiny dots that make up a picture taken by a digital camera. The more of those dots the camera is able to record, the sharper, clearer, and more defined the picture is. (Needless to say, it's more complicated than that, but for our purposes, we can ignore the complications and say that a pixel is a dot, and the more pixels, the better.) That's why early smartphones took fairly unsatisfactory photographs, while the newest ones can take pictures that compare with the work of professional photographers. So a 20–pixel camera takes a very fuzzy, grainy photograph compared with an 8–megapixel or 16–megapixel smartphone camera. The Cornell researchers improved the quality of the pictures their camera takes by clever application of mathematical techniques, but the result is still rather fuzzy and grainy.

But that's not the end of the story.

Scientists at Rice University, Bell Labs, and the University of Glasgow have been experimenting with ways to build up detailed digital photographs using single–pixel cameras. (The actual equipment is quite large, though.) The Glasgow team is even able to build 3D models of the objects being photographed. The three groups of researchers are using somewhat different approaches, but what their work has in common is that their single–pixel cameras all use multiple views, or snapshots, of the scene being photographed, and those separate views are then combined to yield the detailed final picture. [151, 152, 153]

It's a short step from these preliminary steps to single–pixel cameras contained inside the specks of dust we've been talking about. A single such mote of dust, drifting with the wind and taking innumerable pictures of its surroundings, combined with adequate memory and computing power, will be able to build up a detailed picture of those surroundings. A million such motes snapping photos of the same object or scene from innumerable, slightly different angles will build up a remarkably detailed 3D picture. Combining a stream of such images from all of those motes will result in extraordinarily detailed, three–dimensional videos of everything those million motes encounter.

The art of miniaturizing microphones is far more advanced than that of miniaturizing cameras. MicroElectrical-Mechanical System (MEMS) microphones have been available commercially for years and are used in such consumer products as hearing aids. A MEMs microphone is a tiny component of a microchip and is manufactured as part of the chip–manufacturing process.

The smallest MEMS microphones commercially available today would fit comfortably inside our dust motes. [154]

Data Storage

Storing the videos recorded by the coming dust motes will require a lot of data–storage capacity. Moreover, those videos will have to be stored inside those tiny motes, along with a powerful computer and other devices. How feasible is this?

Even apart from the matter of dust motes, recording of data is already a growing problem as the world generates increasing amounts of digital data, especially video recordings. Researchers everywhere are constantly looking for better ways to store such data — better in terms of longevity (the quality of the recorded data doesn't deteriorate over time) and density (the amount of data that can be packed into a given, preferably small, space). One method scientists have long been interested in is data storage in molecules of DNA, the material of which our genes are constructed. A DNA molecule can last for tens of thousands of years without degradation, and each molecule contains an immense amount of information.

Scientists at a bioinformatics research lab in the UK recently managed to create an artificial DNA molecule that contained the data they wanted to record. They were also able to read the data back successfully. This is of course what your computer does with its hard drive, but the DNA method is vastly more dense. (Also vastly more long–lived

— about 10,000 years for the DNA, the researchers estimate, vs. 10 years or so for your hard drive.) The researchers estimate that, using their method, 100 million hours of high–definition video could be stored in about a cup of DNA. [155]

This achievement is an early step. Even so, the data density of this method is impressive. To test their method, the researchers created a clump of DNA molecules containing a recording of Martin Luther King's "I Have a Dream" speech, a photograph of their research institute, a copy of Watson and Crick's famous paper describing the DNA molecule, the complete text of all of Shakespeare's sonnets, and a file describing their encoding method. They described the result as looking like "a tiny piece of dust."

At this point, storing data in molecules of DNA requires physically large equipment and a lot of time. Also, the result is not something that can be simply erased and written over, unlike a computer's hard drive or the memory chips inside a smart phone. Because of its longevity, DNA storage offers great promise for long–term, archival storage of data.

There is great interest in DNA storage, and a lot of time and money being spent on developing it. Perhaps that effort will bear fruit, and smart dust motes of the future will be able to use DNA storage to hold enormous amounts of data.

Even if that never happens, microchips store data, and the continuing shrinking of the size of microchips that we discussed in **Section 4: Diminishing Computers** means that our dust motes will have room for copious storage attached to their powerful, microscopic computers. The only question is whether the amount of data each mote can store will be stupendous or merely astounding.

* * * * *

Looking at this march of miniaturization, we can predict that not too many years from now, private individuals all over the world will be turning out highly sophisticated electronic devices the size of motes of dust, containing tiny but powerful computers and much other minuscule equipment as well.

But why would people want to do that? What will be the purpose of these motes of dust? What will they actually be doing? We'll delve into that in **Section 5: Dust Net World**.

The Best Smart Phone Ever

Mary raised her voice to get John's attention. "Honey, stop playing with your new toy and come eat dinner."

"Okay, okay." Reluctantly, John collapsed the virtual screen and keyboard and put his new phone, now back to its minimal credit–card–sized configuration, in his shirt pocket.

He went into the dining room and sat down in front of the dinner Mary had set out, but he ate mechanically. All through the meal, he talked about his new smart phone. He listed its remarkable specifications — even though he had done so quite a few times before and Mary had tuned him out each time, as she did now.

"I don't even need a computer anymore," John said. "This thing is more powerful than my desktop and my tablet. It's even able to detect a bunch of WiFi networks that don't show up on my tablet. My whole life is on it, and I always have it with me. It's the best smart phone ever."

"It still makes phone calls, doesn't it?" asked Mary, who thought she should say something.

John laughed. "Oh, sure. It's so amazing! Did I tell you that it can ... " On and on he went.

Suddenly he broke off and stared at a fly buzzing above his food.

"Damn," John said. "I think that's the first fly I've seen this summer. Last summer, they were all over the place." He waved it away from his food.

Mary went and got a flyswatter.

"Won't do any good," John said. "Remember? They've evolved. You can't get them."

Mary ignored him, as usual. She moved slowly and carefully toward the fly, which had settled down on the end of table. She raised the flyswatter slowly, positioned it carefully, held her breath. Then she brought it down with a *thwack*.

She raised the flyswatter. A nauseating splatter of fly guts now decorated the table.

"There," she said.

"That's disgusting," John said, taking a picture of the splatter with his phone. "I'm sharing that with everyone I know."

"*You're* disgusting. But you're right about the bugs. They've disappeared. I wish the dust would disappear. It seems like I'm dusting a lot more than I used to, and there's still dust everywhere."

"Maybe it's insect eggs, not dust. Maybe the bugs laid all their eggs and then died."

"Then where are their bodies?" Mary asked.

"Okay, maybe they didn't die. Maybe they all went to Washington. That would explain why there are so many fucking idiots in Congress."

The phrase *fucking idiots in Congress* triggered an alert a thousand miles away. It would have been ignored if not for John's previous IRS audit, which had caused the data stream from his cell phone to always be filtered for a number of trigger words and phrases.

A security tech in the surveillance installation responsible for the region of the country that included the city in which John lived skimmed the previous few minutes of John and Mary's conversation and then listened to the ongoing conversation for a while in real time.

What boring people, he thought. They're no threat.

Just to be sure that they would continue not to be a threat, he accessed John's cell phone and looked at the list of WiFi networks it was showing John. He saw John's home network and the home networks of some of his neighbors. All of them were unsecured. The operator sniggered at that.

He also saw three separate networks with names starting with *DustNet*. None of them required a login. This time, the operator didn't snigger. Instead, he sent a quick message to a different department in his agency to let them know about the presence of those three networks in John's neighborhood. Then he reconfigured John's phone so that it would no longer see or have access to any of the three.

He canceled the alert that had first caught his eye and turned his attention to a new alert that had just popped up on his screen. Somewhere in America, another citizen had said something that tireless, unsleeping software deemed troubling.

5
DUST NET WORLD

We've discussed some political, social, and technical trends that might seem unrelated. Let's review them quickly and see where the combination of these trends is taking us.

Drones are becoming widespread. An increasing number of governments are using them, and at the same time, the use of drones is spreading rapidly in the private sector all over the world. Drones are also evolving. At one extreme, weaponized drones are becoming larger and more fearsome. At the other extreme, surveillance drones are becoming smaller and more able to stay in the air for longer periods; they are also becoming cheaper and increasingly popular with the general public. Autonomous — i.e., independent — operation is beginning to be incorporated into both types of drones.

Governments want to control access to the Internet in order to remain in power. Corporations want to control access to the Internet in order to make lots of money. Both of them can maintain such control only as long as citizens/consumers are forced to access the Internet through a relatively few bottlenecks. Those are the points where government can choke off access. Those are the gateways for the use of which corporations can charge exorbitant fees, and they are the mechanism corporations can use to control Internet content.

Political activists of all kinds need the ability to communicate freely with each other. They also want to get their messages out to the general public. Individuals who don't consider themselves activists nonetheless want to be able to communicate with friends and relatives without feeling that they have to guard their words and without having to worry about the legal consequences if, for example, they verbally attack a corporation. In other words, all of these people want the ability to communicate without fear of corporate and government snooping or control. In the near term, small, private drones serving as WiFi hotspots, combined with peer–to–peer relaying of messages, will provide a way for people to evade government and corporate control over communications.

Video and sound recording devices are becoming remarkably tiny. At the same time, it's common for them to have built–in Internet connectivity. Soon, they'll be small enough to be undetectable. Police won't be able to arrest people for recording them in the act of, say, abusing peaceful protestors because the police won't know which bystander is recording them and simultaneously uploading the video to YouTube. Even without WiFi hotspots embedded in drones, as envisioned above, because of the increasing availability of public WiFi hotspots (for example, in nearby coffee shops) and Internet access via the cell phone network, there are fewer and fewer physical locations where such abuse can take place without recordings being made and uploaded to the Web for the world to see.

There are, of course, still places where frightful abuses can be carried out without the world seeing recordings of the horror — secret CIA torture camps, for example. As we will see, that is going to change.

The trend that draws all of this together is the diminishing size of computers. Microchips have been shrinking for decades and will continue to shrink for years to come.

Perhaps the efforts to create quantum computers will succeed, bringing us immensely powerful computers whose size will be measured in nanometers. But even if that technology never does come to fruition, the powerful small computers we've been talking about are inevitable. Within 10 years or so, they will be small enough to fit inside a speck of dust, with room to spare for data storage, WiFi connections, and sound and video recorders.

Smart Dust

A computer the size of a speck of dust is not a new idea.

For about the last 20 years, researchers in the Defense Department, universities, and private research organizations have been investigating what they call *smart dust*. This dust would consist of a great number of tiny electronic devices, able to communicate with each other by means of WiFi, and scattered over an area to perform various tasks.

At this point, and despite the name, we're not really talking about dust.

Currently, the individual particles of smart dust, called *motes*, are visualized as being around a millimeter across, or about the size of a grain of rice. In the early days, smart dust was envisioned as primarily being used to measure temperatures, chemicals, and so on, although the military's main purpose in pushing the idea of smart dust was to have a way to eavesdrop on an enemy on the battlefield. Nowadays, the tasks envisioned for smart dust have expanded to include monitoring bridges and pipelines and being able to identify individuals and track their movements. If the motes can be made cheaply, and if the problem of providing sufficient electrical power for them to operate can be solved, then the dust could be produced in huge quantities and be scattered on the ground everywhere. [156, 157]

Note that the smart dust motes would be static, not mobile. They would have no way to move themselves, and they would be too large and heavy to be shifted around by anything but a very strong wind. Also, they would not be able to communicate with each other over great distances. Combine this with their lack of mobility, and it's clear that smart dust would only be effective at eavesdropping over a wide area if the individual motes could be produced quickly, cheaply, and in immense numbers.

Technology based on the smart dust concept is already in use. Large numbers of small networked devices are showing up in a number of places, but the devices are still fairly large and designed for limited special purposes.

The technology continues to be developed. The motes are getting smaller and cheaper; one estimate has them costing five cents apiece by 2020. The original vision of innumerable surveillance devices the size of grains of rice is coming closer. [158]

When that original idea of smart dust comes into being, the effect will be profound but one-sided. Smart dust will be a tool for governments and big corporations — a way to gather huge amounts of data about people and things. We private individuals will have no control over the dust. Most of the time, we won't even be aware of it. From our point of view, the physical nature of the dust, while technically interesting, will be irrelevant. The aspect of the dust that will really matter will be its ubiquitousness. We won't care about the size or nature of the eyes and ears constantly watching us. We'll only care that there will be eyes and ears constantly watching us.

Given the continuing miniaturizing trends we've been talking about, it's inevitable not only that smart dust the size of rice grains will come to be, but also that the dust motes will continue to shrink.

Driven by the needs — or at least the desires — of the military, of surveillance and law-enforcement agencies, and of corporations, the motes will eventually become those specks of dust we talked about in **Section 4: Diminishing Computers**. The specks, or motes, will be powerful computers, but they will be much more than that. They will also be equipped for wireless contact with their fellow specks, and they will contain powerful cameras, video recorders, microphones, and a variety of sensors. They may be able to store a fair amount of the data they collect. They will be able to pass the collected data to many other specks, ensuring that the data survives even if the individual speck is destroyed, and that it is passed on along the network of dust specks until it finally reaches its destination: the government or civilian agency or corporate office that controls the specks.

This level of smart dust will be the successor to the gnat–sized surveillance drones we discussed in **Section 1: Diminishing Drones**. It will also make those drones obsolete for most purposes. It will be carried everywhere in the world by the wind. It will go everywhere that natural dust does now, which is more than can be said for the robotic gnats of the near future, and it will be undetectable in places where even a robotic gnat would be seen and stopped.

Just as is already the case with drones, the dust will be produced by many governments and corporations. It will be used to spy on military installations and corporate researchers. Governments and corporations will work frantically to create defensive measures and countermeasures against the dust. Like drones before them, the particles of dust will continue to get smaller.

Motive Power

There will probably be no need for most of these computerized motes of dust to have any control over their own motions. They will drift upon the wind, powerless to change direction or go close to objects or people of interest.

If there are enough of them floating around, and if they are all in constant communication with each other and their home bases, that won't present a problem. At any moment, a large number of motes are sure to be drifting past whatever their human controllers are interested in observing. Each passing mote will get only a brief, fragmentary view of the target, but adding all of those fragments together will yield a complete and detailed narrative. This is a more general version of what we discussed earlier concerning constructing detailed sound and video recordings from innumerable still pictures and sound bites.

There will be times, though, when it will be desirable for a dust mote to have control over its motion.

For example, suppose a handful of dust motes enter a secure facility — perhaps carried by a chance eddy of air as someone walks into the building, or perhaps stuck to the person's clothing or inside his lungs. The mote operators are very interested in seeing what's inside that facility, but thanks to excellent air filters and bad luck, very few motes have entered the building before. Obviously it would be highly desirable for the motes to explore the building in a deliberate way, rather than betting on the chance that air currents within the building will eventually carry them everywhere inside.

Here's another example. It will often be necessary for a dust mote to maneuver close to another mote. This could be for the purpose of secure communication. Nothing could eavesdrop on two motes that are in physical contact and exchanging data directly — unless it's another, similarly equipped mote. Or it could be for purposes of sabotage. Just as there will be hunter–killer drones, a topic we discussed in **Section 1: Diminishing Drones**, there will also be hunter–killer dust motes. We'll talk more about this a bit later.

Because of their tiny size, it will be impractical or even impossible to equip the dust motes with jet engines or rotors, the way current drones are equipped. However, that tiny size makes a different kind of power source entirely practical: the interaction between magnets and the Earth's magnetic field.

The Earth's magnetic field is very weak. It exerts a force on anything magnetic, but it has no visible effect on, say, a refrigerator magnet. The latter is too heavy to be affected by the tiny force exerted on it by the Earth's magnetic field. On the other hand, the magnetic needle of a compass is large enough to be quite visible to the naked eye, and yet it is moved easily by the Earth's magnetic field.

The weight of one of our specks of dust will be insignificant. (The weight of a speck of natural dust is around one millionth of a gram, and our dust motes will have a very similar weight.) If a mote contained a very small, weak magnet, it could use the magnet's interaction with the Earth's magnetic field to move itself quite rapidly.

Appropriately small magnets will be available.

Physicists at Hamburg University in Germany have created the world's smallest stable ferromagnet. It consists of five atoms of iron. Since an atom of iron has a diameter of about a quarter of a nanometer, this means that this tiny magnet is only a bit more than a nanometer across. It would be lost inside our dust mote, or even inside the computer inside our dust mote. [159]

The purpose of the research at Hamburg isn't to construct standalone magnets. The scientists are working toward very small data storage technology. However, their work points the way.

For that matter, it probably won't be necessary for the dust mote to contain tiny physical magnets. Probably much better, and offering much more control, will be electromagnets. The dust motes will be able to use their own power supply to turn their self–contained electromagnets on and off, as needed. These electromagnets will simply be part of the circuitry inside the microchips making up the tiny computers inside the motes.

In practice, the situation will not be that straightforward. For one thing, a dust mote will encounter a lot of resistance due to collisions with real dust and even with molecules of air, so its controlled motion will be slow. For another, sudden gusts of wind will overwhelm the small magnetic force it will use to propel itself. Actual progress will be slow and frequently interrupted by unwanted, random motions. So controlled motion will be reserved for unusual occasions. Most of the time, it will be far more practical to just let the dust motes drift with the wind.

Dust and Other Nets

Within 20 years at the most, but probably 15 years or even less, invisible clouds of manmade dust motes containing computers, sound and video recorders, and significant data-storage capacity will be drifting in the winds and floating on the seas. They will be present almost everywhere in the world. They'll be in the parks, in our workplaces, and in our homes. Thanks to the wind, they'll even be in the most remote wilderness areas. They will drift in the atmosphere, and they will carpet the surfaces of the oceans.

Many of these computer motes will be military devices, gathering intelligence, keeping watch on other countries and on citizens. Many will belong to local law-enforcement agencies and civilian government surveillance agencies. Many will be corporate motes, gathering information designed to make very wealthy people even wealthier. As we've already seen, these machines won't need the Internet. They will form their own networks.

The previous paragraph refers to three categories of these networks of tiny computers. For convenience, let's call them Military Net, Government Net, and Plutocrat Net.

They'll probably communicate with each other in varying degrees. They'll also communicate with their human masters. They won't communicate with or be accessible to the rest of us, the vast majority, the world's private citizens.

This is certainly a grim scenario. This is a prediction of a world in which a constellation of powerful and hidden entities have complete access to every detail of our private lives. We will have no way of knowing which corporation or government agency — military, civilian, law-enforcement — is spying on us at any moment. Nor will we know what they intend to do with the data they gather. This would be the foundation for complete corporate-government control — fascism, in other words, and fascism more complete and thorough than Adolf Hitler and Benito Mussolini ever dreamed of.

Moreover, it is almost certainly coming.

Fortunately, this is only one side of the picture. The development of this system of surveillance and control contains within it the seeds for the development of an opposing system that will, we can hope, limit it and possibly defeat it.

Increasingly, mixed among these clouds of drifting, floating dust–speck computers will be other specks produced by small groups of individuals with no connection to government or to the corporatocracy. Technology, especially electronic technology, behaves that way. Neither the government nor big corporations can keep control of it for long.

This fourth class of dust–speck computers will constitute a fourth world–wide network. Let's call it Dust Net. Instead of repression or profit, its purpose will be to provide ordinary citizens with access to data, news, opinion, and like–minded human beings.

Just like the drone WiFi hotspots we talked about earlier, these dust specks will be accessible from your cell phone or tablet computer or home computer. Thus, most of the world's population will be able to connect to a free worldwide communications network that will completely bypass government restrictions and corporate strangleholds. Dust Net will be an immensely powerful force for freedom.

Dust Net will also be a surveillance tool, but the targets of its surveillance will be politicians, generals, corporate power structures, and the police. Dust Net's motes will be equipped with sound and video recording devices, and what they record will be distributed across the world. This means that torture of prisoners within the most hidden jails or conversations deep within government agencies or corporate headquarters will no longer be secret. They will be known to the world.

None of us will be able to hide from Military Net, Government Net, and Plutocrat Net, but neither will the people in control of those three networks be able to hide from Dust Net.

Unlike the case with Military Net, Government Net, and Plutocrat Net, Dust Net's recordings probably won't be stored in central locations. Those would be far too vulnerable; they would be made to disappear quickly.

However, Dust Net itself would provide the storage. The total data-storage capacity of millions upon millions of Dust Net motes will be immense. Corporations today are moving their data to storage in what is called "the cloud," but Dust Net will be true cloud storage.

Dust Net will evolve to counter the other three networks. It will be intended to spy on the powerful and protect the rest of us. However, its motes won't discriminate. That would require a level of artificial intelligence that we're not likely to see for a long time to come. This means that Dust Net will record everything and everyone. Those floating specks of dust will allow all of us to watch and listen to the self-styled rulers of the world making their plans, but they will also let all of us watch and listen to each other in our most private and intimate moments.

This will mean a social and political upheaval unlike anything the world has experienced before. No place in normal life is truly dust free. It's frightening to think that every moment of your life will be recorded, stored away, and accessible to anyone who cares to view the recording. We'll be living in a global village where all the walls are made of glass.

In a moment, we'll return to this aspect of Dust Net and expand on it a bit. For now, let's consider some larger social consequences of the ubiquitous motes.

Science, it is often said, thrives on openness. True, but innovation thrives on privacy. From the solitary inventor of the past to the academic or corporate researchers of today, innovators are driven by the assurance of possessing the results of their work and profiting from it. For the inventor or corporate researcher, the profit is monetary. For the academic researcher, it can also be monetary, but it's more commonly a published paper and the associated academic credit and career advancement. How will any of this be possible if, thanks to Dust Net, competitors are looking over the researcher's shoulder all the while?

Will creativity in music and literature be stifled for the same reason? Perhaps the only people writing books or music in the future will be those who really and truly do it for love of the art. Dust Net will destroy the chance for profit or fame.

The level of crime will surely drop.

Obviously, conspiracies will be impossible. You won't even be able to plot with a friend to hold up a liquor store, let alone plot with a large group to overthrow a government. Perhaps groups will invent new, secret languages composed of new words or agreed–upon hand signals. However, sophisticated software analysis by law–enforcement computers, using copious data collected by their own intelligent dust motes, will probably decode those new languages fairly quickly.

Despots will no longer bother to imprison or exile political enemies because prisoners and exiles would still be able to maintain constant communication with other enemies of the regime. Assassination will be the only sure way to put a stop to conspiracies. But of course conspirators will be immediately aware of plans to take action against them. Neither conspiracies nor despotisms will be likely to survive for long.

Crimes of passion or madness will still be committed, and presumably at the same rate — or perhaps at a greater rate, if the knowledge of constant eavesdropping drives people mad. Premeditated crimes will only be committed by individuals who make all their plans entirely in their heads. Only stupid criminals will keep notes.

Those crimes that are committed will be quickly solved. Thanks to Government Net, law-enforcement computers will have complete sound and video recordings of the crime as it happens. Other recordings will show where the criminals came from before the crime and where they went afterwards, leading to their rapid capture. Courts will surely allow such recordings as evidence. Convictions will be quick and sure.

A bizarre complication will be the existence of two-way transparency. Law enforcement will be watching criminals even before they commit their crimes, but, thanks to Dust Net, criminals will be watching the police who are investigating and pursuing them. Each side will know what the other is doing. The police, however, will have numbers, organization, and communication on their side. Only criminal organizations of equivalent size and strength will be able to compete with them, and the existence of the surveillance I've been describing will make the creation of such organizations next to impossible. The only way individual criminals or small gangs will be able to avoid capture and prosecution will be to flee, and obviously flight will also be next to impossible.

Thanks to Dust Net, graft, corruption, and collusion will largely disappear. The only people committing those particular crimes will be the ones who are so powerful that they are beyond retribution. Such politicians and plutocrats will be entirely open and honest about their vileness — even more than they are now.

It's hard to see the shape of the end result of all of these forces. Will society settle into some simple form of worldwide, direct democracy, or will it enter a state of constant anarchy? I suspect that we'll see large numbers of temporary associations, not defined by geography, forming to take care of various social needs — *ad hoc* governments, in effect. Conventional governments and national boundaries will fade away. The most organized forces remaining in the world will be corporations, increasingly autonomous armed forces, and increasingly connected intelligence agencies. The rest of us will need Dust Net more than ever.

Weaponization

Once you have a device that can go anywhere and watch any enemy, why stop at surveillance? It's inevitable that some of the motes used in Military Net and Government Net will be weaponized.

Given the size of the motes, they won't be equipped with guns or rockets, of course. It will be sufficient to insert explosives into them. Again, because of their size, the explosives won't be very powerful, but they won't have to be. One mote won't be able to damage a building or an artillery piece by exploding inside it. However, a great number of motes, packed together and exploding simultaneously, will be a different matter. Such an explosion will be devastating inside a computer.

The more obvious use of exploding motes will be as tools of assassination. In the future world we're talking about, every breath you take will draw in these motes in large numbers. It wouldn't take much of an explosion to kill you.

Small explosions are crude and unreliable tools, though. It's likely that instead of explosives, some motes will contain extremely powerful poisons. Once one of them is anywhere inside your body — in your lungs, or, if it's small enough, in your blood stream — your survival will be completely under the control of whoever controls the mote.

No leader will be safe, and that includes corporate leaders.

Assassination won't be limited to the top of the ladder, however. Inevitably, private individuals will follow the government, military, and corporate lead. Killer motes will become part of Dust Net, too. Private grievances will be resolved in the most final way possible. The only barriers to a flood of murders will be the certainty of punishment and the knowledge that your potential victim might have been forewarned — that is, if he happened to be watching you at the right time.

This is a recipe for anarchy. Or perhaps it will turn out to be a recipe for very thorough democracy and painstaking honesty. Perhaps the resulting society will be extraordinarily friendly and polite; we'll all learn to smile a lot. We won't know which of those paths we're going down until we're already some distance along it.

A less blunt weapon will be a laser. A team of researchers at Northwestern University has created a laser about equal in size to a virus — considerably smaller than our dust motes. [160]

Lasers of this sort may be available eventually for our dust motes, and they may be powerful enough to do some damage on a microscopic scale at extremely close quarters. If that never proves to be possible, the more reliable destructiveness of explosives and poisons will still be available.

Countermeasures

Of course there will be continuing attempts to fight this surveillance.

The obvious first step will be to create dust–free environments.

These already exist. The factories in which semiconductors are produced are dust free, as was described in **Section 4: Diminishing Computers**. The same is true of the clean rooms in which vehicles are built that will be sent to explore other planets. This is done to avoid contaminating other worlds with earthly microorganisms. [161]

You might think that politicians or corporate managers who are plotting something they don't want the general public to know about would simply meet in such a clean room. No dust specks of any kind would be able to get in, be they spies for another corporation or government agency, a foreign government, or the people.

However, when you look at any photograph of technicians working in a clean room, something jumps out. The people are all wearing special clothing designed to protect the items they're working with from contamination *from the human beings*. In some cases, their outfits amount to space suits — in this case, designed to keep the damaging environment in instead of out.

That's fine for manufacturing microchips or assembling Mars landers. It will be ineffective as protection against surveillance dust motes. Unless the surveillance target — in this case, the corporate or government manager — was born and lived his entire life in a completely dust–free environment, there will be dust on his skin and in his nose and lungs. Most of that will be normal dust, but some of those specks of dust will be motes from Military Net, Corporate Net, Government Net, and, best of all, Dust Net. Any extreme measures to eliminate those motes would probably kill the man.

If that man were to meet with his fellow conspirators in a dust–free clean room, he could wear a special suit to keep the dust on and in his body from contaminating the room, but that will do no good. He has to be able to communicate with the people he's meeting with, and the surveillance dust motes on his body will pick up and record all of those sounds and sights.

Perhaps in addition to being dust free, the meeting room will be impervious to radio waves, so that the dust motes will be unable to communicate with their network while the man is inside the room. That will be pointless. At some point, he'll have to leave the room. Then communication will again be possible, and the motes will be able to report what they've recorded. For that matter, even if he spends his time in a building that radio waves can't penetrate, as soon as he exhales outside the special room, some of the motes from his lungs will float freely in the breeze. They will encounter fellow motes from their own network, at which point they will pass on what they've recorded. Those motes in turn will do the same. It may take a while, but eventually the incriminating recordings will reach the people the conspirators don't want them to reach.

One anti–mote weapon that might be somewhat effective would be an EMP generator.

An EMP, or electromagnetic pulse, is an intense burst of electromagnetic energy. EMPs are produced by nuclear explosions, as well as in other ways, and they can burn out electronic equipment. Because our society is becoming ever more dependent on such equipment, there is the fear that an enemy could detonate a powerful nuclear warhead high above the United States, counting on the resulting EMP to paralyze the country and its military forces. Electronic communications and computers would be wiped out.

Such an EMP would surely destroy the electronics contained in surveillance dust motes, as well. Of course, this would be an absurd weapon for any government to use over its own territory as a way to destroy those motes. However, nuclear explosions are not the only way to produce EMPs. It's possible to build a small electronic gadget that produces an EMP with very limited reach. In fact, you can find instructions on the Web for building crude versions of EMP generators.

Instead of relying on a dust–free clean room, therefore, it would make more sense to install EMP generators in the meeting room to kill any dust motes that entered.

This is problematic, however. EMPs are not selective. They destroy electronic devices without choosing which ones to destroy. That would include the conspirators' cell phones and watches. Of course, that would be just a minor inconvenience. The EMPs bathing the meeting room would also destroy the hearing aids that some of the conspirators would probably be wearing. That would be a not–so–minor inconvenience.

As we've seen, the conspirators would bring in surveillance motes inside their bodies, in their lungs and nasal passages, so the EMP would have to be powerful enough to penetrate into the conspirators' lungs. That would result in the destruction of cardiac pacemakers — a very major inconvenience, indeed. Conspiratorial meetings would have to be limited to conspirators with good hearing and good hearts.

Perhaps the technology of EMP generators will evolve to the point where the EMPs they produce will destroy only surveillance motes and nothing else. If so, they could be used everywhere, and not just in hidden meeting rooms. Unwanted surveillance motes would be eliminated. However, the motes in the various networks we've referred to — Government Net, Military Net, Plutocrat Net, and Dust Net — will be fairly indistinguishable physically, and their electronics will probably be identical. Only their software will differ. Therefore, any EMPs sweeping all public spaces will disable the motes owned by governments and corporations along with those spying on governments and corporations on behalf of citizens.

Some governments and corporations might consider that worthwhile. In effect, they would be able to return the areas under their control to the pre–Dust Net era. Losing their own surveillance capability might strike them as a small price to pay for escaping the eyes and ears of the public.

But this assumes no countermeasures. Whether you're talking about human armies on the battlefield or infectious microorganisms and the human immune system, the history of warfare is a story of the constant synergistic evolution of offense and defense, of new defensive technology being devised to counter new offensive technology, which then in turn evolves in an attempt to overcome the new method of defense. The cycle never ends. This cycle will also apply to surveillance dust and the defensive measures taken against it.

Given the growing urge to keep feeding data to government and corporate databases, new models of dust specks would be developed that would be immune to the carefully tuned EMPs. The technology behind those new models would migrate quickly to Dust Net. Once again, those microscopic eyes and ears would be everywhere.

I mentioned that the various types of motes would be physically identical or highly similar. The differences would lie mainly in their software. This suggests that a software attack would have a greater chance of success than the EMP route.

Attacks against software systems (e.g., viruses, trojan horses, denial of service attacks) and the defenses mounted against those attacks are subject to the same synergistic evolutionary cycle experienced by all other offense–defense systems. Dust mote software will evolve to counter attacks against dust motes. In response, the software attacks will become more sophisticated. The cycle will repeat.

At any point in the cycle, software attacks will have only limited success. Here's why.

One of the classic examples of the co–evolution of attack and defense technology is the side–by–side development of the architecture of castles during the Middle Ages and the development of better ways to attack those castles. As more powerful weapons and tactics were invented to batter down the walls of the castles, castles were built with ever thicker and sturdier walls. Moats were added to keep attackers from getting too close.

The history of the changes in castles and the weapons and methods used to attack them is complex, and there's no need to delve into it. For our purpose, here is the important part of the story.

The force attacking a castle had three primary ways to win the fight and conquer the castle. The first was to have accomplices on the inside who would open a door and let the attackers in. The second was to besiege the castle for long enough that the defenders would run out of food and water and be forced to surrender or try to escape. The third was to batter down the walls, or at least damage them sufficiently in one or more places that the attackers could force their way inside. On the level of dust motes and software, the constant evolution of attack and defense is analogous to the third situation.

Now imagine how daunting the attackers' task would have been if the defenders had been able to receive a steady stream of stones and mortar from the outside, along with stonemasons who repaired the damage to the walls as quickly as the attackers could inflict it.

Surveillance motes will be able to do exactly that in response to software attacks. The stonemasons will be the vast numbers of their fellow motes that they will constantly encounter as they drift in the winds. The stones and mortar will be the software contained in those fellow motes. When motes from a given network — Dust Net, let's say — encounter each other, which will happen constantly, they will identify each other using the same kind of encrypted methods already in use for financial and other secure transactions on the Internet. This will include an exchange of encryption keys, so that no other mote will be able to eavesdrop. They will exchange their stored data and video records (limited, perhaps, by how much data-storage is available in each mote). They will also compare their internal software. The mote (or handful of motes) whose software differs from that of the others in the group will be assumed to have suffered software corruption, either accidental or deliberate. The software will be reloaded from the unaffected motes. If that can't be done, then the corrupted mote will be recorded as unreliable and thereafter excluded from the network.

This is a fairly clumsy, crude, and time–consuming approach, and better techniques will surely be developed, just as castle defenses kept evolving. However, the immense redundancy resulting from the sheer number of dust motes in the network will probably remain the key to defeating software attacks.

So a crude physical attack, such as EMP generators, and software attacks, such as viruses, won't work. To keep those unwanted motes from snooping, something better will be needed.

In **Section 1: Diminishing Drones**, we talked about the inevitable development of hunter–killer drones — gnat–sized drones designed to find and destroy other gnat–sized drones. In the same way, the most effective defense against unwanted surveillance dust motes will be dust motes whose function is not surveillance but the identification and destruction of other dust motes.

Destruction will be the simple part of the hunter–killers' mission. A minute amount of explosive material attached to the target mote would do the trick. Or the hunter-killers could be equipped with EMP generators that they could use to fry the targets' electronic components. None of the limitations we talked about for the use of EMP generators would apply here, because the minuscule generator would be right next to the target and the EMP pulse would have a very limited range.

Identification will be trickier. It will certainly be extremely important. There must be almost no chance of the hunter-killers destroying motes that are part of their own networks. Visual identification won't be reliable; camouflage will be far too easy. Hunter-killers won't be able to rely on eavesdropping on the data exchanges between a target mote and other motes because of the encryption mentioned above.

Instead, hunter-killers will approach their potential prey directly and attempt to establish communications. The motes from their own networks will respond correctly. Like human spies, fellow spies on the same side will know the signals. Any other mote will not respond correctly and will be attacked.

This approach is too simplistic, though. Under this scenario, the hunter-killers will be destroying motes of all other networks but their own, including the networks belonging to allies. Clearly, the methods used by motes to identify each other as allies will have to be quite sophisticated. It will also have to be possible to change those methods quickly to reflect changing alliances between the motes' human masters — i.e., shifting alliances between corporations or nations. This also implies that those human masters will have to be able to change the programming of existing motes. Recalling them to the factory won't be feasible. Some way will have to be developed to transmit signals to the existing motes that will change their settings and modify their software. Making sure that those transmissions cannot be intercepted or mimicked and also that the motes won't respond to reprogramming transmissions from an enemy organization will introduce an extraordinary level of complexity to the operation of these networks and to the design and programming of the motes.

All of this will be subject to the same synergistic coevolution of attack and defense — in this case, challenge and response — we talked about above. I think we can safely predict that the mote industry will become a significant employer all over the world.

Cracking the encrypted handshake used by motes — the initial conversation they will use to recognize other motes as part of their own network — might not be all that difficult. Even now, the type of attack–defense synergistic coevolution we've talked about is underway between the design of encrypted systems (e.g., for financial transactions) and would–be thieves trying to break into those systems. The NSA has supposedly found a way to crack even advanced encryption, but the NSA, naturally, is not sharing their breakthrough with anyone. For everyone else, the key to breaking into those highly secured systems is sufficient computer power. Fortunately, the required level of computer power is not available outside a very few labs. Unfortunately, as we've seen, computer power continues to increase steadily and dramatically, and the computer power needed to crack the most secure, highly encrypted systems will eventually be widely available. An individual dust mote won't have that kind of computer power, but a large number of them, networked together, will. Therefore, an individual hunter–killer mote won't be a serious threat, but a swarm of them will be unstoppable.

So, after all, it may be possible to attack and eliminate just those dust motes belonging to a specific network. However, it may not be the most cost–effective way to undermine and disarm an opposing network. An indirect attack will probably prove more cost effective. Why not mimic the recruitment of human enemy agents, who are often "turned," meaning that they switch sides, bringing their talents, skills, and training with them? Instead of destroying functioning, well designed dust motes, it would be far better to subvert them, to detach them from the enemy's network and make them part of your own.

The result will be that the various networks will be in a constant state of flux. Motes will switch sides frequently. Which network has the most motes and hence the most relative power will be constantly changing.

This will actually be a good thing for the general public, for otherwise Dust Net would be at a severe technological disadvantage and would be destined for eventual elimination. Homemade dust motes would be unlikely to be able to avoid destruction by the hunter–killers produced by multibillion–dollar corporations and government agencies. When the warfare is waged at the software level, however, we have seen repeatedly that non–government, non–corporate software developers, such as the "hacktivists" who operate under the name Anonymous, can compete very well with their government and corporate rivals. If anything, Dust Net should be more successful at recruiting motes to its side than the other networks will be.

Rossum's Universal Robots

The motes of all the networks will be operating within a constantly changing and very challenging environment. They will encounter numerous attempts via software to disable or recruit them. They will be subject to evolving techniques of electronic warfare or straightforward physical attacks from hunter–killer motes. Many times a second, a mote will encounter another mote and will have to be able to recognize it as friend or foe. They will have to record sound and video under constantly changing conditions (for example, changing natural light and background noise levels throughout the day) or due to naturally occurring interference (for example, actual dust, which will be far more bothersome to them than it is to us).

Constantly updating the motes' software from afar to counter or predict all of these conditions won't be feasible. Often, it won't even be possible. Many of the motes will be out of contact at any one time; they may be drifting inside radio–wave–proofed buildings or lifted by winds so high into the atmosphere that they are out of radio signal range.

Therefore, there will be a constant effort to make the motes more autonomous — able to adapt to their surroundings and make quick judgments. They may not achieve true artificial intelligence, the ability to think for themselves in the way that humans do, but as their software and tiny computers become ever more powerful, the argument about how intelligent they truly are will become increasingly academic.

This will parallel the growing trend of autonomy for all of our electronic servants. At some point, we'll have to ask ourselves whether our gadgets are mindless servants or self–aware equals. That will be the point at which we'll begin to fear that they will become our masters, if we don't fear that prospect already.

This is not a new idea. The great science fiction author Isaac Asimov explored it in depth in his robot stories and novels. He was far from the first. In 1920, the year Asimov was born, the Czech author and playwright Karel Capek wrote a play titled *Rossum's Universal Robots*, in which he introduced the word *robot*. The play, often referred to as *R.U. R.*, also introduced the idea of a robot revolt — in the play, a successful revolt.

Unlike our future smart refrigerators and vacuum cleaners, the dust motes we're discussing will frequently cluster or clump together in huge numbers, and those clusters will possess huge computer power. If eventually some kind of motive power is added to the dust motes — i.e., the ability to control their own motions rather than being under the control of the wind — then the robot revolt Capek envisioned could be real, but at the microscopic level.

We shouldn't worry about highly intelligent clouds of dust motes attacking human beings, though. Whether those clouds are under human control or are thinking for themselves, a more important target for them will be other motes and other clouds of motes.

This war may well be coming, but in that fight, human beings will be insignificant. We'll be mere bystanders. Unfortunately, when a war is under way, huge numbers of innocent bystanders become — in the deliberately dispassionate language of military planners — collateral damage. Fortunately, dust motes, even clouds of them, will be more precise with their targeting than Predator drones seem to be.

The exception will be the people and computers in charge of Military Net, Government Net, and Plutocrat Net, as well as all the variations of those networks in various countries. They will all be very high-value targets, and their death toll will probably be very high, perhaps approaching 100%. No one will be in charge of Dust Net, by its very nature. Therefore, if this War of the Motes does happen, the result is likely to be the destruction of the other three networks, or at least the severe diminution of their power. They will be liberated from human control and direction and reduced to doing what their autonomous software enables them to do.

The thought of millions upon millions of partially self-aware dust motes, operating as individuals and in clusters, many of them armed, drifting around the world without any human control, is not a comforting one. Let's hope that the ability of the Dust Net to recruit and absorb these orphaned motes will be such that, in the end, there will only be Dust Net, and perhaps a very few unaffiliated individual motes. That might be too optimistic, though.

The War of the Motes will involve every weapon available, from direct physical attacks by one mote upon another to software attacks. As has always been true in war, the weapons and the defenses used against them will evolve rapidly as the fighting continues.

Perhaps the war will be sparked by some relatively minor incident — the mote equivalent of the assassination of the Archduke Ferdinand that set off the terrible destruction of World War One. As with human wars, the fighting will draw in forces — in this case, dust–mote networks — that were not involved at the beginning. Corporate, military, and civilian government mote networks from all over the world will create rapidly changing alliances. This will be a truly world war.

It will also probably be a very quick war. Imagine if World War One had not been fought by huge armies separated from each other by No Man's Land, but rather by millions of individual soldiers scattered evenly across the battlefields, with each man attacking the nearest enemy soldier as soon as he saw him. The death toll would still have been horrifying, but the war would have lasted for a few days instead of more than four years. The worldwide War of the Motes will probably take just a few hours, perhaps just minutes.

Because the war will be waged at the microscopic level, it will be far below our level of perception. We are likely to be unaware of it, although we will be unnerved by the virtually simultaneous deaths of large numbers of government and corporate leaders all over the world. While we watch those shocking announcements on our television sets, a silent war of immense consequence will rage all around us, far beneath the horizon of our senses.

Private Lives

As we discussed above, privacy won't just be greatly diminished by Dust Net. It will be eliminated. What small amount of privacy escaped those gnat–sized drones will not escape the eyes and ears of the motes.

You won't be alone when you're sleeping or on the toilet or in the shower or having sex. If you take illegal drugs, you won't be alone while you're doing so. Oh, there will be a slight possibility that you will be alone during those times. After all, most of us are not really worth watching most of the time. But you will have to assume that someone, or perhaps millions of someones all over the world, are curious enough or bored enough to be watching you and listening to you. Even if no human being is watching, the motes will be watching and listening, and they will be recording for posterity everything they see and hear. Presumably, posterity won't be interested in the details of the lives of the great majority of us, but we will always be aware that the recordings exist. Anyone who wants to will be able to observe any second of our lives that they feel a passing interest in.

Our advanced technology will have taken us back to the time of our pre–human ancestors. We'll be a worldwide group of primates living in a pack in a worldwide forest, with everyone fully aware of what everyone else is doing all the time.

This is a creepy picture for us, but presumably people who grow up in such a world will have very different ideas about privacy and private lives than we do. It will seem natural to them that the only privacy people will have will be within their thoughts.

But perhaps even that is optimistic.

Since the 1970s, medical researchers have been investigating and developing what are known as Brain Computer Interfaces, or BCIs. These are devices that connect the brain to a computer. The technology has progressed from an electroencephalograph machine (the technology that gave rise to BCIs) to a small device that can be implanted in the brain, transmits its signals wirelessly from the brain, and can be recharged wirelessly from outside the body. [162, 163]

The computer to which a BCI is attached interprets the brain's signals and takes some action, such as controlling a prosthetic device. As that implies, one of the main aims of this research is to replace lost arms and legs with prosthetic limbs that the patient can control very accurately and easily with his thoughts. BCIs will probably eventually reach the point where a completely paralyzed person can wear a prosthetic suit and control it with his mind, so that he will be able to live an almost normal life.

There is no reason to limit the control exerted by the brain through a BCI to prosthetic limbs. Scientists in the UK are developing a system that might eventually let astronauts control the flight of their spaceship using just their minds. 164

In a down–to–earth and very topical application, Chinese scientists have demonstrated brain control of a small drone. 165

The other use of BCIs is in brain research.

Remarkable progress has already been made, using BCIs and other technology, in understanding how the brain processes thoughts and images and how those relate to the signals transmitted to the computer by the BCI.

Japanese scientists used a fluorescent probe to observe and interpret the firing of different neurons in the brain of a fish. This should help researchers determine which brain circuits are involved in various complex behaviors. 166

Working directly with human subjects, scientists at Cornell University used functional magnetic resonance imaging to measure changes in blood flow in the subjects' brains. At the same time, the subjects were asked to imagine various scenarios involving specific fictional people. The researchers were able to determine from their brain readings which fictional character each subject was thinking about while imagining the various scenarios. 167

Carnegie Mellon University scientists used functional magnetic resonance imaging (fMRI) to determine with great accuracy the relationship between patterns of brain activity in human subjects and specific emotions. [168]

Scientists in Japan conducted magnetic resonance imaging (MRI) scans of subjects' brains as they were falling asleep. The subjects were immediately awakened and asked to describe what they had been dreaming. Images seen in the dreams were entered in a database together with the MRI patterns of the subjects' brains taken while they were dreaming. Once a large database had been built up, scientists were able to use MRI scans of sleeping subjects' brains to predict with 60% accuracy what images the subjects were dreaming about. [169]

University of California researchers have created small, very thin, flexible devices called electronic tattoos that can be stuck on the skin, can read brain activity, and can communicate with each other wirelessly. One fascinating possible use of electronic tattoos has to do with subvocalization. This refers to the movements your throat muscles make when you think about talking, even if you don't actually make a sound. If electronic tattoos are attached to the throat, they can detect and interpret these movements. Potentially, they could wirelessly transmit to another person what you're thinking about saying without you actually making a sound. This would give us all a practical version of telepathy. [170]

These are all baby steps, to be sure, but these results are remarkable, nonetheless.

Research will continue and progress will continue to be made. Perhaps someday, motes of dust belonging to Dust Net and the other networks, nestled in our hair, will be able to read our minds. Even the last refuge from surveillance, the last place where we can be safe from eavesdropping, will have been taken from us. We don't know, at this point, if this is even possible. We can be sure, though, that if it is possible, it will almost certainly happen.

Even without mind reading, dust motes sitting on the skin of our throats might be able to pick up our subvocalized speech in the same way as the electronic tattoos described above and then transmit our unspoken words across Dust Net to motes in someone else's ears, where they would be transformed into sounds. Unstoppable, worldwide communication would no longer require smartphones or other mobile devices, and it would be silent.

If advertisers still exists in the world of Dust Net, they will fall in love with one aspect of this method of communication: the ability to make sounds in people's ears and perhaps images on the surfaces of their eyes. If you think commercials are intrusive now, imagine having them show up, unwanted and unstoppable, in your ears and eyes at any time of the night or day. That could lead to an upsurge in the number of assassination dust motes.

John and Mary, Alone at Last

Displaying a level of patience that would once have been impossible for him, John asked Mary once more if she would like to go for a walk.

Mary stared into space and said nothing, as usual. The only change John could see was that her expression became even more terrified. She had been falling into these weird fits ever since she'd become convinced that people were watching her all the time.

"No one's watching you," John would tell her.

"They're listening, too," she would say. Then she would retreat to their bed and sit with her legs tucked up against her, her arms around her legs, her chin resting on her knees, and stare into space, shivering slightly, seemingly oblivious to him and the rest of the world.

"A walk would do you good," John said, but he knew she couldn't hear him. Or wouldn't hear him. It amounted to the same thing.

He sighed, went downstairs, got his light jacket from the hall closet, and went out alone. Maybe she'd snap out of it before he got home. That had happened before.

It was Saturday afternoon, so John wasn't surprised that the street was empty of traffic, both vehicular and pedestrian. He was sorry about the emptiness, though. Mary's withdrawal, which seemed worse this time than usual, had made him yearn for human company. He headed for the park. It was a cool day, but sunny, and he knew there'd be people there.

There were, but not as many as he'd expected.

He walked down one of the winding paths. The tall trees whose branches met overhead and the lush grass on both sides of the path usually lifted his spirits, but not today.

He didn't see anyone else walking. He saw a few people sitting on the benches beside the path. Some of them were staring into space in much the same way Mary did. It gave John the shivers. Others were talking to themselves. Sometimes they smiled or laughed or nodded. That was even creepier than the ones who said nothing. Craziness was proliferating, John thought.

He passed a group of children playing on the grass. They were running around, chasing each other, shouting, laughing. They, at least, were behaving normally. He stopped to watch them.

After a while, he realized that their motions weren't random. They were playing some sort of game. He wondered what it was. For a while, he watched, trying to figure out the purpose of the game. He failed.

It was strange. The kids seemed to be moving in complex, changing patterns, as though they were communicating with each other. But they were laughing and shouting wordlessly. He couldn't even see that they were using some sort of hand signaling method. And yet they moved in harmony.

It was too confusing. After a while, John gave up and continued walking.

The park seemed like an alien place today. It was as though he had somehow been transported to another planet. It was not a comforting thought, and the park was not a comforting place.

For quite a while, he was alone. There were no people around him, young or old. He realized that there were no mosquitoes, either. Usually, even on a day as cool as this, they were abundant, and they usually seemed particularly drawn to him. John had no idea why there weren't any in the park today, but he was grateful to whatever was keeping them away.

He encountered a young couple walking toward him on the path. They were holding hands and gazing into each other's eyes. He stepped aside to let them pass. They moved on, oblivious to his presence.

He smiled as he watched them. They were reenacting the old, eternal story. Watching them walk away, he felt happy.

And then he felt sad. He remembered when he and Mary had walked together that way — although they had actually talked to each other, not just gazed into each other's eyes. This young couple seemed to have a serious communication problem right here at the beginning of their relationship. But that was beside the point. Even though they were silent, watching them made him miss those happy, early days. And thinking about the way he and Mary had talked to each other back then made him even sadder at the way she was behaving now.

Not that he communicated much with the world in general, or ever had, John thought as he walked on. He had always felt apart from others and not able to make real contact with them. Freddy, one of John's coworkers, always talked about how he was constantly making new friends all over the world thanks to the latest technology. Freddy talked too much and too loudly and too quickly. He was an example of too much communication. John sometimes wondered what Freddy was talking about. How was he making friends all over the world? It made no sense.

The world often made no sense to John. He worked hard but kept falling further behind financially, and he was living in a society that seemed more alien to him all the time. This was a train of thought that often possessed him. It always made him angry, and it was doing so today. The only way to get rich is to rob a bank, he thought.

He stopped walking. Rob a bank! Why did I think that? What a stupid idea. I bet I could do it, though. No, not a bank. They're too well guarded. Maybe a jewelry store. Or a liquor store. Something like that. That would be easier and safer.

He walked along smiling, lost in this new speculation. He began to think seriously about weapons and disguises and plans and getaways.

A spring entered his step. He was tired of his old life. He needed a new one. The idea of becoming a holdup man had a strange appeal.

I bet I could collect a lot of money in a short time, he thought. Then Mary and I could go somewhere completely new. Maybe it would do her good.

However, the thought did not do John much good. His speculations triggered an alarm in a faraway data center. He had two strikes against him in the database already, so the software escalated the alarm instead of doing nothing, as it would have with someone else.

Another layer of software evaluated John's current thoughts and the records of his two previous transgressions. The calculation yielded a risk index of 50.01%. Given a number like that, a human being might have been inclined to let the matter slide, but the software was dispassionate. The index was over 50 percent, and that was that. The termination order was given.

A few dozen of the many motes nestled comfortably inside John's lungs were designed for a special purpose. Upon receipt of the termination order, they broke apart into even tinier pieces, releasing their minuscule store of a potent, slow–acting poison.

By the time John went to bed, the poison had begun to accumulate in his heart. Some time after he gave up trying to get Mary to talk to him and closed his eyes to sleep, the poison had reached a fatal level. John fell asleep quickly. His heart slowed and then stopped forever.

Mary was still sitting on her side of the bed, in the same position as before, wide awake, and staring into space. She had not yet snapped out of her fit.

John's death was confirmed, and he was deleted from the relevant databases.

Mary never did snap out of her fit. She remained where she was, next to John's body and oblivious to it. Over the next couple of days, she added the smell of her defecation and urination to the increasing odor of John's decay. By the end of the week, she had died of thirst.

A different kind of alert was sent to the watching software, and Mary, too, was deleted from a number of databases. For the first time in a long time, no one was watching her or listening to her.

No one official, at any rate. Recordings of her protracted and unpleasant death were popular for a while among people with a penchant for that sort of thing. In death, she became a minor celebrity. That celebrity faded after a few weeks as recordings of more horrible deaths climbed the charts.

People were always dying, and other people were always watching.

6
AFTERTHOUGHTS

Emergent Behavior

The networks we have been talking about will be complex and evolving systems of immense numbers of sophisticated computers. Large systems of interacting components often behave unexpectedly, in ways that could not have been predicted from the nature of the individual components. The system itself exhibits this unexpected behavior. This characteristic is called *emergent behavior* or *emergence.* Dust Net and the other networks will almost surely display emergent behavior.

There's nothing supernatural or mystical about this. We don't need to invoke some kind of group mind or artificial intelligence soul to explain it. It's just that the interactions between the individual components can never be completely predicted or mathematically modeled, and the more components there are, the more complex and unpredictable their group behavior becomes. Nonetheless, we keep building large systems of all kinds and dealing with the problem of emergent behavior. Generally speaking, emergent behavior has been manageable so far, or at least its effects are not significant or dangerous.

Dust Net, Government Net, Military Net, and Plutocrat Net will take the size of server networks to a new level. It's a fair bet that the emergent behavior that will arise in them will not always be innocuous or insignificant. It may also not be manageable. We won't know until we get there. Or perhaps we won't know. If one or more of these microscopic networks becomes truly intelligent, it might have no interest in us or our doings. It might go on about its business, whatever that is, without us having any idea that this has happened. As long as the network keeps providing us with the services we expect from it, we won't know what else it's doing. An intelligent network would probably want to keep it that way.

Alien Net

Or the plural, Alien Nets.

Stories in which a technologically superior race of aliens invades the earth have a long history, which is usually traced back to the H. G. Wells novel *The War of the Worlds*, published in 1898. This type of story has moved from the printed page to the movie screen, with big-budget alien–invasion movies appearing regularly. The level of acting and writing rarely matches the high quality of the special effects, but many of these movies are quite successful at the box office, testifying to the continuing scary appeal of the basic idea.

That idea no longer seems all that fanciful.

As we discover more planets circling suns other than our own, the estimated number of Earth–sized planets in our galaxy capable of supporting life keeps going up. The latest estimated number is 100 billion. That immense number makes it seem very likely that there are very many highly advanced alien races in the galaxy — perhaps many millions of them. A large percentage of those millions is bound to be far more advanced than we are. And a large percentage of those advanced races is bound to be as aggressive and bloodthirsty as the worst of the alien invaders in the movies, or even more so.

Fortunately, the odds are that they all live a long, long way from us — much too far away to make invasion likely. Although some scientists and engineers continue to investigate ways to travel at speeds greater than the speed of light, most physicists don't think it will ever be possible. Of course, highly advanced aliens may well have tricks up their sleeves that are far beyond our capabilities, and to make matters worse, they may have many more sleeves than we do. But we can probably breathe easily and spend more time worrying about crazy nations on Earth than crazy aliens in space.

Above, I used a simple numerical argument to conclude that there are probably a great number of aggressive and bloodthirsty alien races scattered across the galaxy. The same calculation leads us to conclude that there are probably just as many peaceful, benign, really very nice alien races out there whom it would be a pleasure to get to know. We won't get to know them because of those same immense distances that protect us from the awful aliens.

However, they might get to know us. They might already have done so.

If, as I have been arguing, we are not many years away from the inevitable appearance of Dust Net, Military Net, Plutocrat Net, and Government Net, then surely all those technologically advanced alien races must already be beyond that point, probably far beyond it. Whatever effect those dust networks had on their societies, it must all have reached a stable state by now. The dust has settled.

For an advanced, peaceful, scientifically inquisitive race, the dust networks will be invaluable tools for acquiring knowledge about their own world and other worlds. The distances between the stars, in most parts of the galaxy, may make it impossible for living aliens to travel to other planetary systems, but they would be very likely to send unmanned probes out. We do the same thing within our own Solar System. It's our way of gathering knowledge about distant planets that humans may never visit in person. Instead of probes like ours, wonders of technology to our eyes but surely laughably primitive to the eyes of highly advanced aliens, they would be more likely to send probes packed with something much like Dust Net across the interstellar gulfs.

This would probably have little appeal to the bloodthirsty races. The only reward would be knowledge, and even that would take an immense time to be returned to the home world. The outward journey would take centuries, or thousands of years, or even millions of years.

The probes that survived that trip and found worlds worth investigating at the end of the trip would have to successfully establish their Dust Nets on the target worlds. The great quantities of data gathered by those alien networks would then have to be sent back home, another journey of hundreds or thousands or millions of years. That return trip would have to be made in the original probes. If the original probes were no longer operational, new probes would have to be constructed by the network motes themselves, or by automated manufacturing facilities created by the motes, or by factories owned by the native races of the target worlds and controlled by the alien motes. In addition to wanting knowledge of other worlds and other races for its own sake, the civilizations sending out the original probes would have to take the very, very long view.

So we probably don't have to worry about an alien invasion. Nor are aliens likely to be here already, hiding among us. There is a pretty good chance, though, that alien versions of Dust Net are already here. Fortunately for us, they were most likely sent by peaceful, inquisitive alien races who are interested in watching us and recording our doings.

If there is one such alien net already here, then there are probably very many of them. This follows from the same numerical argument that leads us to the conclusion that great numbers of alien civilizations probably exist. Presumably, they would be able to detect each other and interact with each other. Presumably, those interactions have been peaceful and cooperative and will continue to be so.

There was no flying saucer crash in Roswell, New Mexico, and the U. S. government does not have a repository of alien technology extracted from such a vessel. However, if we could capture and dismantle an alien Dust Net mote, our own technology would surely take a huge leap forward. The alien motes would probably be equipped to prevent this, but even if our motes were to do no more than detect the presence of alien intelligent motes, the effect on us would be profound. That is, it would be profound if the motes doing the detecting were Dust Net motes. If they were Plutocrat Net, Military Net, or Government Net motes, the rest of us would never hear anything about it. The Roswell mythology might end up coming true.

Other Avenues

Maybe none of this will happen.

Maybe Dust Net and those other networks will never exist. Technological prognostication is notoriously difficult and unreliable. For centuries, people have been writing detailed descriptions of what the future will look like, predictions that seemed logical and inevitable to the writers, and usually breathtaking and amazing to their readers, but that now seem quaint or even ludicrous to us. The technological pathways that seem inevitable turn out to be the ones that society does not take, while other avenues, ones that seemed unlikely or that no one thought of, end up being the ones that shape the world.

For example, suppose that a surprising, hitherto unsuspected physical phenomenon is discovered that makes it possible to use every surface as a camera and microphone. The surveillance aspect of the dust networks we've been talking about would immediately become real. Depending on the nature of the phenomenon, so would the communications aspect of those networks. The technology would be different, but the end result would be the same. Privacy would disappear and everyone would be able to talk to everyone else.

We don't need to hypothesize some sort of new physics, however. Trends already underway may make Dust Net and the other dust–based networks unnecessary and may keep them from ever coming to be.

Increasingly powerful computer circuits and microchips are being integrated into everything from home appliances to clothing. These are usually distinguished by the adjective "smart" — smart clothing, smart fabrics, smart refrigerators, etc. Many of the smart appliances come with built–in Internet connectivity. For example, you can already buy an Internet–connected garage–door opener so that you can check via the Internet to make sure that you closed your garage door when you left home. You might prefer an Internet–connected washing machine — now available — which allows you to start a load of laundry with a voice command spoken into your smart phone while you're still at work. Smart clothing, still being developed, will be able to monitor your vital signs and summon help if you have a medical emergency.

This has been called "the Internet of Things," but it's not just "things" in the usual sense that are getting connected to the Internet.

Under development at the University of Strathclyde is a paint that can detect structural damage in buildings, bridges, wind turbines, etc., and transmit a warning using wireless communication. [171]

Given the trends we discussed in **Section 2: Diminishing Privacy**, it's clear where all of this is headed. Computer circuitry connected to the Internet is being embedded in everything to provide any number of useful services and capabilities to consumers and engineers, but an inevitable side effect of this trend is the spread of surveillance. Intended for benign or beneficial purposes, this hardware will become a major tool in the collection of immense quantities of data about everyone, and the data will be stored forever in the huge databases we talked about earlier.

This is an extension of what is already happening with drones, and it is equivalent to what I predicted will happen because of the dust–based networks.

However, there is one important difference between this world of surveillance based on the ubiquitousness of embedded circuitry and the world of Dust Net.

In Dust Net world, there is no privacy. The prying eyes and ears of government and corporations are everywhere. But so are the prying eyes and ears of private citizens. In addition, there is complete, unfettered communication everywhere and between everyone. That is, there's a balance. The system works in both directions. They watch us, and we watch them. Everyone is forced to be honest.

In embedded computer circuitry world, surveillance and control go in one direction only, and the bonus of free communication does not exist. Only governments and their corporate allies will have access to the stream of surveillance data. Citizens will be under constant observation, but government officials and plutocrats will be free of it. At least, they won't be observed by us. Also, since we won't have access to the numerous networks formed by the plethora of embedded computer circuitry, we won't be able to use them for communication with other citizens. This would be a world in which the great mass of humanity would be under the complete control of an elite.

For all the uncomfortable aspects of Dust Net world, that is still the world we should hope for.

The Final Destination

The only thing we can be sure of is that a world of total surveillance is coming rapidly. We don't know if the surveillance will be one way or two way. We don't know if the benefit of free, worldwide communication will also be part of this world. All we do know is that, fairly soon, privacy will no longer exist. No walls will shut out the all–seeing eyes and the all–hearing ears. Every single detail of our lives, no matter how trivial or humiliating, will be observed and stored away for possible later review.

This is not the exciting world of the future most of us have envisioned. It is, however, the world that is coming. We'd best prepare ourselves for it.

REFERENCES

1

"EXCLUSIVE: CIA didn't always know who it was killing in drone strikes, classified documents show" NBC News, June 5, 2013. http://openchannel.nbcnews.com/_news/2013/06/05/18781930-exclusive-cia-didnt-always-know-who-it-was-killing-in-drone-strikes-classified-documents-show

2

"China's New Drones Raise Eyebrows" The Wall Street Journal, November 18, 2010.
http://online.wsj.com/article/SB10001424052748703374304575622350604500556.html

3

"China Has Drones. Now What?" Foreign Affairs, May 23, 2013. http://www.foreignaffairs.com/articles/139405/andrew-erickson-and-austin-strange/china-has-drones-now-what

4

"France in talks with U.S., Israel to buy drones: minister" Reuters, May 19, 2013. http://www.reuters.com/article/2013/05/19/us-france-drones-idUSBRE94I04H20130519

5

"Prototype of European Combat Drone Makes Maiden Flight" Defense News, December 1, 2012.
http://www.defensenews.com/article/20121201/DEFREG01/312010003/Prototype-European-Combat-Drone-Makes-Maiden-Flight

6
"British stealth drone to undergo first test flight" The Telegraph, January 13, 2013.
http://www.telegraph.co.uk/news/uknews/defence/9797738/British-stealth-drone-to-undergo-first-test-flight.html

7
"Alarms raised over lack of military drone pilot training" The Telegraph, December 11, 2012.
http://www.telegraph.co.uk/news/uknews/9737112/Alarms-raised-over-lack-of-military-drone-pilot-training.html

8
"Driving drones can be a drag" Eurekalert, November 14, 2012.
http://www.eurekalert.org/pub_releases/2012-11/miot-ddc111412.php

9
"A future for drones: Automated killing" The Washington Post, September 19, 2011. http://articles.washingtonpost.com/2011-09-19/national/35273383_1_drones-human-target-military-base

10
"UN expert demands moratorium on killer 'robot' weapons" The Raw Story, May 30, 2013.
http://www.rawstory.com/rs/2013/05/30/un-expert-demands-moratorium-on-killer-robot-weapons/

11
"Activists launch campaign against 'autonomous weapons': Killer robots must be stopped" The Raw Story, February 24, 2013.
http://www.rawstory.com/rs/2013/02/24/activists-launch-campaign-against-autonomous-weapons-killer-robots-must-be-stopped/

12
"Frontex chief looks beyond EU borders" EU Observer, January 14, 2013. http://euobserver.com/fortress-eu/118471

13
"EU countries look to joint spending on drones" EU Observer, February 13, 2013 http://euobserver.com/tickers/119057

14
"European defense firms ask governments to launch drone programs" The Raw Story, June 16, 2013.
http://www.rawstory.com/rs/2013/06/16/european-defense-firms-ask-governments-to-launch-drone-programs/

15
"EU and Israel research crime–stopping drones" EU Observer, February 7, 2013 http://euobserver.com/justice/118951

16
"Turkey to manufacture armed version of national drone" Today's Zaman, July 18, 2012. http://www.todayszaman.com/news-286926-turkey-to-manufacture-armed-version-of-national-drone.html

17
"Iran showcases cyber, drone warfare skills" The Hindu, January 1, 2013. http://www.thehindu.com/news/international/iran-showcases-cyber-drone-warfare-skills/article4262659.ece

18
"Israel Downs UAV With Dogfighting Missiles" Defense News, October 7, 2012.
http://www.defensenews.com/article/20121007/DEFREG04/310070002/Israel-Downs-UAV-Dogfighting-Missiles

19
"U.S. moves to sell advanced spy drones to South Korea" Yahoo! News, December 25, 2012. http://news.yahoo.com/u-moves-sell-advanced-spy-drones-south-korea-195243564.html

20

"US selling combat drones to undisclosed countries" RT, May 7, 2012. http://rt.com/usa/news/us-vanguard-drone-foreign-747/

21

"Drones should be included in arms reduction treaties, says medical charity" The Guardian, October 12, 2012.
http://www.guardian.co.uk/world/2012/oct/13/drones-arms-reduction-treaties

22

"German police foil Islamist terror plot to use remote controlled aircraft filled with explosives as guided missiles" Daily Mail, June 25, 2013.
http://www.dailymail.co.uk/news/article-2347946/German-police-foil-Islamist-terror-plot-use-remote-controlled-aircraft-filled-explosives-guided-missiles.html

23

https://www.eff.org/sites/default/files/filenode/20120416_FAA_Drones_COA_0.pdf

24

"Homeland Security Wants to More Than Double Its Predator Drone Fleet Inside the US, Despite Safety and Privacy Concerns" Electronic Frontier Foundation, November 20, 2012.
https://www.eff.org/deeplinks/2012/11/homeland-security-wants-more-double-its-predator-drone-fleet-inside-us-despite

25

"FBI admits to using surveillance drones over US soil" The Guardian, June 19, 2013.
http://www.guardian.co.uk/world/2013/jun/19/fbi-drones-domestic-surveillance

26

"Push to step up domestic use of drones" San Francisco Chronicle, November 27, 2012. http://www.sfgate.com/nation/article/Push-to-step-up-domestic-use-of-drones-4064482.php

27

"Newly Released Drone Records Reveal Extensive Military Flights in US" Electronic Frontier Foundation, December 5, 2012. https://www.eff.org/deeplinks/2012/12/newly-released-drone-records-reveal-extensive-military-flights-us

28

"Push to step up domestic use of drones" San Francisco Chronicle, November 27, 2012. http://www.sfgate.com/nation/article/Push-to-step-up-domestic-use-of-drones-4064482.php

29

"Push to step up domestic use of drones" San Francisco Chronicle, November 27, 2012. http://www.sfgate.com/nation/article/Push-to-step-up-domestic-use-of-drones-4064482.php

30

"Newly Released Drone Records Reveal Extensive Military Flights in US" Electronic Frontier Foundation, December 5, 2012. https://www.eff.org/deeplinks/2012/12/newly-released-drone-records-reveal-extensive-military-flights-us

31

"Drones go mainstream" CNN, January 9, 2013. http://money.cnn.com/2013/01/09/technology/drones/index.html

32

http://www.amazon.com/Parrot-AR-Drone-Quadricopter-Controlled-Android/dp/B007HZLLOK/

33

http://www.indiegogo.com/robotdragonfly

34

"The Next Gun Debate? Armed Drones Could Be Protected By the Second Amendment" US News, May 21, 2013.
http://www.usnews.com/news/articles/2013/05/21/the-next-gun-debate-armed-drones-could-be-protected-by-the-second-amendment

35

"Scientists say: Give drones a chance" Yahoo News, May 29, 2013.
http://news.yahoo.com/blogs/ticket/drone-scientists-hope-change-public-image-124633937.html

36

"WWF plans to use drones to protect wildlife" The Guardian, 2/7/2013 http://www.guardian.co.uk/environment/2013/feb/07/wwf-wildlife-drones-illegal-trade

37

"German railways to test anti-graffiti drones" BBC News, May 27, 2013. http://www.bbc.co.uk/news/world-europe-22678580

38

"Studying Hurricanes With Swarms of Smart Drones" Slate, June 7, 2013.
http://www.slate.com/blogs/future_tense/2013/06/07/hurricane_research_drones_small_autonomous_submarine_and_plane_are_future.html

39

"NASA Sends Unmanned Aircraft to Study Volcanic Plume" Jet Propulsion Laboratory, April 1, 2013.
http://www.jpl.nasa.gov/news/news.php?release=2013-119

40

"US Army Developing Robo-Snake Technology" Armed Forces International, February 28, 2012. http://www.armedforces-int.com/news/us-army-developing-robo-snake-technology.html

41

"Sea-surfing 'wave glider' robot deployed to help track white sharks in the Pacific" Eurekalert, August 16, 2012.
http://www.eurekalert.org/pub_releases/2012-08/blsu-sg081512.php/

42

"Robotic fish to patrol for pollution in harbours" BBC News, May 22, 2012. http://www.bbc.co.uk/news/science-environment-18062235

43

"Realistic Robot Carp Created: First Robot Fish With Autonomous 3-D Movement in Asia" Science Daily, June 26, 2013.
http://www.sciencedaily.com/releases/2013/06/130626113027.htm

44

"Anticipating domestic boom, colleges rev up drone piloting programs" NBC News, 2/29/2013.
http://openchannel.nbcnews.com/_news/2013/01/29/16726198-anticipating-domestic-boom-colleges-rev-up-drone-piloting-programs

45

"70,000 Drone-Related Jobs Anticipated in Next Three Years" Politix, March 12, 2013. http://politix.topix.com/homepage/5069-70-000-drone-related-jobs-anticipated-in-next-three-years

46

"Pentagon develops a flexible, self-camouflaging 'Squid-bot'" The Raw Story, August 17, 2012.
http://www.rawstory.com/rs/2012/08/17/pentagon-develops-a-flexible-self-camouflaging-squid-bot/

47

"Micro-drones will 'hide in plain sight'" Salon, Feb 19, 2013. http://www.salon.com/2013/02/19/micro_drones_will_hide_in_plai n_sight/

48

"NRL Shatters Endurance Record for Small Electric UAV" NRL News, May 9, 2013. http://www.nrl.navy.mil/media/news-releases/2013/nrl-shatters-endurance-record-for-small-electric-uav

49

http://www.draganfly.com/uav-helicopter/draganflyer-x8/applications/government.php

50

"Analysis: Taser-related deaths in US accelerating" The Raw Story, September 5, 2010. http://www.rawstory.com/rs/2010/09/05/taser-related-deaths-accelerating/

51

"Global Opinion of Obama Slips, International Policies Faulted" Pew Research, June 13, 2012. http://www.pewglobal.org/2012/06/13/global-opinion-of-obama-slips-international-policies-faulted/

52

"American public has few qualms with drone strikes, poll finds" The Christian Science Monitor, June 3, 2013. http://www.csmonitor.com/USA/Military/2013/0603/American-public-has-few-qualms-with-drone-strikes-poll-finds

53

"Texas civil libertarians have eye on police drones" Houston Chronicle, October 31, 2011. http://www.chron.com/news/houston-texas/article/Texas-civil-libertarians-have-eye-on-police-drones-2245644.php

54
"CHAMP - lights out" Boeing Corporation, October 30, 2012.
http://www.boeing.com/Features/2012/10/bds_champ_10_22_12.ht
ml

55
"Halton police find $744K worth of drugs using high-tech pot-spotting drones" National Post, December 9, 2013.
http://news.nationalpost.com/2012/09/13/halton-police-find-744k-worth-of-drugs-using-high-tech-pot-spotting-drones/

56
"U.S. Turns to Drones to expand Fight against Drugs in the Caribbean" The New York Carib News, July 18, 2012.
http://www.nycaribnews.com/news.php?viewStory=2265

57
"U.S. ABP & U.S. drones flying over Mexico detecting military drug/human traffickers" Examiner, October 20, 2012.
http://www.examiner.com/article/u-s-abp-u-s-drones-flying-over-mexico-detecting-military-drug-human-traffick

58
"Cell Phone Location Tracking Public Records Request" American Civil Liberties Union, March 25, 2013.
http://www.aclu.org/protecting-civil-liberties-digital-age/cell-phone-location-tracking-public-records-request

59
"Poll: 45% approve of Obama's handling of the economy" CBS News, February 12, 2013. http://www.cbsnews.com/8301-250_162-57568828/poll-45-approve-of-obamas-handling-of-the-economy/

60
"Israel says it knocked out Hamas drone program" CBS News, November 16, 2012. http://www.cbsnews.com/8301-202_162-57551216/israel-says-it-knocked-out-hamas-drone-program/

61

"The NSA's metastasised intelligence-industrial complex is ripe for abuse" The Guardian, June 23, 2013.
http://www.guardian.co.uk/commentisfree/2013/jun/23/nsa-intelligence-industrial-complex-abuse

62

"DOJ: We don't need warrants for e-mail, Facebook chats" CNET, May 8, 2013. http://news.cnet.com/8301-13578_3-57583395-38/doj-we-dont-need-warrants-for-e-mail-facebook-chats/

63

"Judge orders Google to comply with FBI's secret NSL demands" CNET, May 31, 2013. http://news.cnet.com/8301-13578_3-57587003-38/judge-orders-google-to-comply-with-fbis-secret-nsl-demands/

64

"U.S. gives big, secret push to Internet surveillance" CNET, April 24, 2013. http://news.cnet.com/8301-13578_3-57581161-38/u.s-gives-big-secret-push-to-internet-surveillance/

65

"FBI lobbying US government for 'back doors' into Facebook, Google and Skype" computing.co.uk, May 1, 2013.
http://www.computing.co.uk/ctg/news/2265418/fbi-lobbying-us-government-for-back-doors-into-facebook-google-and-skype/page/1

66

"Judge OKs FBI Tracking Tool That Tricks Cellphones With Clandestine Signal" Slate, May 9, 2013.
http://www.slate.com/blogs/future_tense/2013/05/09/stingray_imsi_catcher_judge_oks_fbi_use_of_controversial_tool_in_daniel.html

67

"Dutch police may get right to hack in cyber crime fight" BBC News, May 2, 2013. http://www.bbc.co.uk/news/world-europe-22384145

68

"UK "snoopers charter" pits privacy against security" Reuters, March 26, 2013. http://www.reuters.com/article/2013/03/26/us-britain-security-ralph-idUSBRE92P0D520130326

69

"Sworn Declaration of Whistleblower William Binney on NSA Domestic Surveillance Capabilities" Public Intelligence, July 10, 2012. http://publicintelligence.net/binney-nsa-declaration/

70

"The NSA Is Building the Country's Biggest Spy Center (Watch What You Say)" Wired, March 15, 2012.
http://www.wired.com/threatlevel/2012/03/ff_nsadatacenter/

71

"City Is Amassing Trove of Cellphone Logs" The New York Times, November 26, 2012.
http://www.nytimes.com/2012/11/27/nyregion/new-york-city-police-amassing-a-trove-of-cellphone-logs.html?hpw&_r=0

72

"The End of Privacy?" The New York Times, July 14, 2012.
http://www.nytimes.com/2012/07/15/opinion/sunday/the-end-of-privacy.html

73

"Uncovering License Plate Scanners: The Next Big Thing in Government Tracking" ACLU, Aug 3, 2012.
http://www.aclu.org/blog/technology-and-liberty-national-security/uncovering-license-plate-scanners-next-big-thing

74
"Police Across U.S. Quietly Turning to Cameras That Track All Vehicles' Movements: Survey" Slate, January 14, 2013.
http://www.slate.com/blogs/future_tense/2013/01/14/automatic_lice nse_plate_readers_survey_shows_most_u_s_police_agencies_plan. html

75
"Report: Global Network of Government Spyware Detected in U.S., Authoritarian Countries" Slate, March 13, 2013.
http://www.slate.com/blogs/future_tense/2013/03/13/finspy_from_g amma_group_detected_around_the_world_says_citizen_lab_report. html

76
"The NSA Is Building the Country's Biggest Spy Center (Watch What You Say)" Wired, March 14, 2012.
http://www.wired.com/threatlevel/2012/03/ff_nsadatacenter/all/1

77
"BIG BROTHER'S LISTENING" The Daily, December 10, 2012.
http://www.thedaily.com/article/2012/12/10/121012-news-bus-audio-surveillance/

78
"5 Things You Should Know About the FBI's Massive New Biometric Database" AlterNet, January 8, 2012.
http://www.alternet.org/story/153664/5_things_you_should_know_about_the_fbi%27s_massive_new_biometric_database

79
"The new totalitarianism of surveillance technology" The Guardian, August 15, 2012.
http://www.guardian.co.uk/commentisfree/2012/aug/15/new-totalitarianism-surveillance-technology

80
"Big Brother is watching more than ever" Tampa Bay Times, December 25, 2012.
http://www.tampabay.com/opinion/editorials/big-brother-is-watching-more-than-ever/1267546

81
"U.S. Terrorism Agency to Tap a Vast Database of Citizens" The Wall Street Journal, December 13, 2012.
http://online.wsj.com/article/SB10001424127887324478304578171623040640006.html#project%3DNCTCguideemail%26articleTabs%3Darticle

82
"President And Congress Extend FISA Wiretapping Act To 2017" NPR, December 28, 2012. http://www.npr.org/blogs/thetwo-way/2012/12/28/168220266/congress-extends-fisa-wiretapping-act-to-2017-awaits-obamas-signature

83
"Poll Finds Strong Acceptance for Public Surveillance" The New York Times, April 30, 2013.
http://www.nytimes.com/2013/05/01/us/poll-finds-strong-acceptance-for-public-surveillance.html?pagewanted=all&_r=0

84
"A hidden world, growing beyond control" The Washington Post, July 19, 2010. http://projects.washingtonpost.com/top-secret-america/articles/a-hidden-world-growing-beyond-control/

85
"NTU invention allows clear photos in dim light" Eurekalert, May 30, 2013. http://www.eurekalert.org/pub_releases/2013-05/ntu-nia053013.php

86
"Can Your Smartphone See Through Walls? Engineers Make Tiny, Low–Cost, Terahertz Imager Chip" Science Daily, December 10, 2012.
http://www.sciencedaily.com/releases/2012/12/121210120408.htm

87
"Using WiFi to see through walls" Extreme Tech, August 3, 2012.
http://www.extremetech.com/extreme/133936-using-wifi-to-see-through-walls

88
"US military app uses smartphone cameras to spy" CNET Australia, October 10, 2012. http://www.cnet.com.au/us-military-app-uses-smartphone-cameras-to-spy-339341965.htm

89
"Drones With Facial Recognition Technology Will End Anonymity, Everywhere" Business Insider, May 27, 2013.
http://www.businessinsider.com/facial-recognition-technology-and-drones-2013-5

90
"Hidden Government Scanners Will Instantly Know Everything About You From 164 Feet Away" Gizmodo, July 10, 2012.
http://gizmodo.com/5923980/the-secret-government-laser-that-instantly-knows-everything-about-you

91
"Software Predicts Criminal Behavior" ABC News, August 22, 2010.
http://abcnews.go.com/Technology/software-predicts-criminal-behavior/story?id=11448231

92

"Raytheon Riot Software Predicts Behavior Based on Social Media" PC Magazine, February 12, 2013.
http://www.pcmag.com/article2/0,2817,2415340,00.asp

93

"Clear as ... paper? Scientists 'see' through solid layers" Phys.org, Nov 7, 2012. http://phys.org/news/2012-11-paper-scientists-solid-layers.html

94

"U.S. Army Eyes Super-Small Surveillance Drones" Earth Imaging Journal http://eijournal.com/industry-insights-trends/u-s-army-eyes-super-small-surveillance-drones

95

"Spy-Butterfly: Israel developing insect drone for indoor surveillance" RT.com, May 18, 2012. http://rt.com/news/israel-drone-indoor-butterfly-672/

96

"Robotic insects make first controlled flight" Eurekalert, May 2, 2013.
http://www.eurekalert.org/pub_releases/2013-05/hu-rim050113.php

97

"China tightens internet controls" The Guardian, December 28, 2012. http://www.guardian.co.uk/world/2012/dec/28/china-tightens-internet-controls

98

"Google's dropped anti-censorship warning marks quiet defeat in China" The Guardian, January 7, 2013.
http://www.guardian.co.uk/technology/2013/jan/04/google-defeat-china-censorship-battle

99
"China trying new form of 'Internet censorship' ahead of Tiananmen Square crackdown anniversary" The Raw Story, Jun 1, 2013. http://www.rawstory.com/rs/2013/06/01/china-trying-new-form-of-internet-censorship-ahead-of-tiananmen-square-crackdown-anniversary/

100
"China to boast world's most advanced internet" SmartPlanet, March 29, 2013. http://www.smartplanet.com/blog/bulletin/china-to-boast-worlds-most-advanced-internet/16303

101
"Iran creating software to control social networking websites" The Raw Story, January 6, 2013.
http://www.rawstory.com/rs/2013/01/06/iran-creating-software-to-control-social-networking-websites/

102
"Iran readies domestic Internet system, blocks Google" Reuters, September 23, 2012. http://www.reuters.com/article/2012/09/23/net-us-iran-internet-national-idUSBRE88M0AO20120923

103
"Iran to crack down on web censor-beating software" The Raw Story, June 10, 2012. http://www.rawstory.com/rs/2012/06/10/iran-to-crack-down-on-web-censor-beating-software/

104
"Pakistan bans Facebook and YouTube" Financial Times, May 21, 2010.
http://www.ft.com/cms/s/2/8fdc66cc-643e-11df-8618-00144feab49a.html

105
"Tajikistan orders Twitter ban" The Raw Story, December 22, 2012.
http://www.rawstory.com/rs/2012/12/22/tajikistan-orders-twitter-ban/

106
"Ethiopia clamps down on Skype and other internet use on Tor"
BBC, June 15, 2012.
http://www.bbc.co.uk/news/technology-18461292

107
"Saudi Arabia blocks Viber messaging service" BBC News, June 6,
2013. http://www.bbc.co.uk/news/world-middle-east-22806848

108
"Pakistan blocks cell phone service amid ongoing protests over anti-Islam video" CBS News, September 21, 2012.
http://www.cbsnews.com/8301-503543_162-57517498-503543/pakistan-blocks-cell-phone-service-amid-ongoing-protests-over-anti-islam-video/

109
"Nervous Kremlin seeks to purge Russia's internet of 'western'
influences" The Guardian, April 15, 2012.
http://www.guardian.co.uk/technology/2012/apr/15/kremlin-purge-russia-internet-western-influences

110
"Russians Selectively Blocking Internet" The New York Times,
March 31, 2013.
http://www.nytimes.com/2013/04/01/technology/russia-begins-selectively-blocking-internet-content.html?_r=0

111
"Singapore to regulate Yahoo, other online news sites" Reuters,
May 28, 2013. http://www.reuters.com/article/2013/05/28/net-us-singapore-internet-idUSBRE94R0G220130528

112
"Cellphones blocked in SF to hinder transit protest" Associated Press, August 13, 2011. http://news.yahoo.com/cellphones-blocked-sf-hinder-transit-protest-041114962.html

113
"When Will the Rest of Us Get Google Fiber?" MIT Technology Review, February 4, 2013.
http://www.technologyreview.com/news/510176/when-will-the-rest-of-us-get-google-fiber/

114
"Good-Bye to Seattle's Free Wi-Fi" Community Broadband Networks, May 8, 2012.
http://www.muninetworks.org/content/good-bye-seattles-free-wi-fi

115
"Cyber Intelligence Sharing and Protection Act" Wikipedia. http://en.wikipedia.org/wiki/Cyber_Intelligence_Sharing_and_Protection_Act

116
"CISPA approved in House despite online freedom objections" SC Magazine, April 27, 2012. http://www.scmagazine.com/cispa-approved-in-house-despite-online-freedom-objections/article/238602/

117
"Google vs. God" Slate, August 21, 2012.
http://www.slate.com/articles/double_x/doublex/2012/08/hasidic_jews_and_the_internet_a_bad_combination_.html

118
"The Endless Potential of Flying Robots" Yahoo! News, April 5, 2012.
http://news.yahoo.com/blogs/this-could-be-big-abc-news/endless-potential-flying-robots-190703624.html

119

"ARPANET" Wikipedia. http://en.wikipedia.org/wiki/ARPANET

120

"Tunisia, Egypt, Miami: The Importance of Internet Choke Points" The Atlantic, January 28, 2011.
http://www.theatlantic.com/technology/archive/2011/01/tunisia-egypt-miami-the-importance-of-internet-choke-points/70415/

121

"Free Speech is Only as Strong as the Weakest Link" Electronic Frontier Foundation
https://www.eff.org/free-speech-weak-link#home

122

Global Censorship Chokepoints https://globalchokepoints.org/

123

"Peer-to-peer" Wikipedia http://en.wikipedia.org/wiki/Peer-to-peer

124

"Encrypted and obfuscated? Your P2P protocol can still be IDed" ars technica, August 25, 2010. http://arstechnica.com/tech-policy/2010/08/encrypted-and-obfuscated-your-p2p-protocol-can-still-be-ided/

125

"Wireless ad hoc network" Wikipedia.
http://en.wikipedia.org/wiki/Wireless_ad-hoc_network

126

"Understanding Ad Hoc Mode" Wi–Fi Planet, August 23, 2002.
http://www.wi-fiplanet.com/tutorials/article.php/1451421

127

"MANES: a Mobile Ad hoc Network Emulation System"
http://whispercomm.org/manes/

128

"A Mobile Ad Hoc Network Implementation for Android
Smartphones" Rochester Institute of Technology
http://www.cs.rit.edu/~djf4044/ms/flanagan_research_proposal.pdf

129

"Mobile Ad Hoc Networks: An Evaluation of Smartphone
Technologies" Defence R&D Canada, October 2011.
http://www.dtic.mil/dtic/tr/fulltext/u2/a555594.pdf

130

"samizdat" Encyclopedia Britannica.
http://www.britannica.com/EBchecked/topic/520512/samizdat

131

"The Iranian Revolution" Nonviolent Conflict, April 2009.
http://www.nonviolent-conflict.org/index.php/movements-and-
campaigns/movements-and-campaigns-
summaries?sobi2Task=sobi2Details&sobi2Id=23

132

"What happens when computers stop shrinking?" Salon, March 19,
2011. http://www.salon.com/2011/03/19/moores_law_ends_excerpt/

133

"Exactly how cheap can computers get?" apc Magazine, March 12,
2009.
http://apcmag.com/exactky-how-cheap-can-computers-get.htm

134
Losi 1/36 Xcelorin Brushless Motor (10250kV)
http://www.amainhobbies.com/product_info.php/cPath/1_221_1358
/products_id/18651/n/Losi-1-36-Xcelorin-Brushless-Motor-
10250kV

135
"World's Smallest Electric Motor Made from a Single Molecule"
Science Daily, September 5, 2011.
http://www.sciencedaily.com/releases/2011/09/110904140353.htm

136
"California's first 3D printer retail store to sell $600 model" Ars
Technica, September 21, 2012.
 http://arstechnica.com/business/2012/09/californias-first-3d-printer-
retail-store-to-sell-600-model/

137
"20 Amazing Creations You Can Make With 3D Printing"
HONGKIAT.COM http://www.hongkiat.com/blog/3d-printings/

138
"Untethered Hovering Flapping Flight of a 3D-Printed Mechanical
Insect" Richter and Lipson, MIT Press.
http://mitpress.mit.edu/sites/default/files/titles/alife/0262290758cha
p139.pdf

139
"New Technique May Open Up an Era of Atomic-scale
Semiconductor Devices" NC State University Newsroom, May 22,
2013. http://news.ncsu.edu/releases/wms-cao-mos2/

140
"Researchers Develop Single-Atom Transistor" PC Magazine,
February 21, 2012.
http://www.pcmag.com/article2/0,2817,2400523,00.asp

141
"Jeff Forshaw: quantum computers are leaping ahead" The Observer, May 5, 2012.
http://www.guardian.co.uk/science/2012/may/06/quantum-computing-physics-jeff-forshaw

142
"Particle Sizes" The Engineering Toolbox.
http://www.engineeringtoolbox.com/particle-sizes-d_934.html

143
"All the World's a Stage ... for Dust" NASA Science, June 26, 2001.
http://science.nasa.gov/science-news/science-at-nasa/2001/ast26jun_1/

144
"Scientists Create World's Smallest Microchip" redOrbit, December 14, 2010.
http://www.redorbit.com/news/technology/1966110/scientists_create_worlds_smallest_microchip/

145
"Semiconductor fabrication plant" Wikipedia.
http://en.wikipedia.org/wiki/Semiconductor_fabrication_plant

146
"Microchips are found just about everywhere" Los Angeles Times, December 28, 2010.
http://articles.latimes.com/2010/dec/28/business/la-fi-microchips-20101228

147
"NI LabVIEW Microprocessor SDK"
http://sine.ni.com/nips/cds/view/p/lang/en/nid/201953

148
"Printing tiny batteries" EurekAlert, June 18, 2013.
http://www.eurekalert.org/pub_releases/2013-06/wifb-ptb061813.php

149
"Air Power: New Device Captures Ambient Electromagnetic Energy to Drive Small Electronic Devices" Georgia Tech Research News, July 7, 2011. http://www.gtresearchnews.gatech.edu/device-captures-ambient-energy/

150
"Cornell University's microscopic camera makes photos with mathematics" Engadget, July 7, 2011.
http://www.engadget.com/2011/07/07/cornell-universitys-microscopic-camera-makes-photos-with-mathem/

151
"Compressive Imaging: A New Single-Pixel Camera" Rice University. http://dsp.rice.edu/cscamera

152
"Bell Labs creates lensless single-pixel camera" Digital Photography Review, Jun 4, 2013.
http://www.dpreview.com/news/2013/06/04/bell-labs-creates-lensless-single-pixel-camera

153
"Researchers build one-pixel cameras that can take 3D pictures" Wired UK, May 22, 2013.
http://www.wired.co.uk/news/archive/2013-05/22/one-pixel-camera

154
"World's smallest MEMS mic debuts" EE Times, Marcy 30, 2011.
http://www.eetimes.com/electronics-news/4214610/World-s-smallest-MEMS-mic-debuts

155
"Researchers Make DNA Data Storage a Reality: Every Film and TV Program Ever Created -- In a Teacup" Science Daily, Jan 23, 2013.
http://www.sciencedaily.com/releases/2013/01/130123133432.htm

156
"Smart Dust" Computerworld, March 24, 2003.
http://www.computerworld.com/s/article/79572/Smart_Dust

157
"Future World – Smart Dust Micro Computers"
http://www.youtube.com/watch?v=GvdGggusRYU

158
"Smart Dust" University of Houston ISRC Technology Briefing, March 2005.
http://www.bauer.uh.edu/uhisrc/ftb/smart%20dust/smart%20dust.pdf

159
"Physicists construct world's smallest magnet composed of only five iron atoms" Nanowerk, January 4, 2013.
http://www.nanowerk.com/news2/newsid=28282.php

160
"Researchers Create Laser the Size of a Virus Particle" Northwestern University, November 5, 2012.
http://www.northwestern.edu/newscenter/stories/2012/11/researchers-create-laser-the-size-of-a-virus-particle.html

161
"Methods And Implementation" NASA Office of Planetary Protection http://planetaryprotection.nasa.gov/methods

162
"Wireless, implanted sensor broadens range of brain research" Eurekalert, Mart 19, 2013.
http://www.eurekalert.org/pub_releases/2013-03/niob-wis031913.php

163
"Brown University creates first wireless, implanted brain-computer interface" Extreme Tech, March 4, 2013.
http://www.extremetech.com/extreme/149879-brown-university-creates-first-wireless-implanted-brain-computer-interface

164
"Steer a spaceship with your brain? It's a thought" NBC News, Mar 7, 2013. http://science.nbcnews.com/_news/2013/03/07/17225162-steer-a-spaceship-with-your-brain-its-a-thought

165
"Thought-controlled quadcopter takes to the skies" New Scientist, August 30, 2012.
http://www.newscientist.com/blogs/onepercent/2012/08/thought-controlled-quadcopter.html

166
"This is what a fish thought looks like" Eurekalert, January 31, 2013.
http://www.eurekalert.org/pub_releases/2013-01/cp-tiw012313.php

167
"Mental Picture of Others Can Be Seen Using fMRI, Finds New Study" Science Daily, March 5, 2013.
http://www.sciencedaily.com/releases/2013/03/130305091000.htm

168
"Press Release: Carnegie Mellon Researchers Identify Emotions Based on Brain Activity" Carnegie Mellon News, June 19, 2013. http://www.cmu.edu/news/stories/archives/2013/june/june19_identif yingemotions.html

169
"Scientists 'read dreams' using brain scans" BBC News, April 4, 2013. http://www.bbc.co.uk/news/science-environment-22031074

170
"Temporary tattoos could make electronic telepathy and telekinesis possible" Txchnologist, February 19th, 2013. http://txchnologist.com/post/43496630304/temporary-tattoos-could-make-electronic-telepathy

171
"Nanotech-enhanced "smart paint' promises to detect structural damage" engadget, 30th January, 2012. http://www.engadget.com/2012/01/30/nanotech-enhanced-smart-paint-promises-to-detect-structural-da/

ABOUT THE AUTHOR

David Dvorkin was born in 1943 in Reading, England. His family moved to South Africa after World War Two and then to the United States when David was a teenager. After attending college in Indiana, he worked in Houston at NASA on the Apollo program, then in Denver on the Viking unmanned Mars lander. His aerospace career ended in 1974. Since then, he has worked as a software developer and technical writer. He and his wife, Leonore, have lived in Denver since 1971.

In addition to non–fiction, David has published a number of science fiction, horror, and mystery novels. He has also coauthored two science fiction novels with his son, Daniel. For details, as well as quite a bit of non-fiction reading material, please see David's Web site, *http://www.dvorkin.com.*

David is on Facebook at
http://www.facebook.com/DavidDvorkin
and on Twitter at
http://twitter.com/David_Dvorkin.